THE GUINNESS STORY

This edition first published 2016 by The O'Brien Press Ltd.
12 Terenure Road East, Rathgar, Dublin 6, Ireland.
Tel: +353 1 4923333; Fax: +353 1 4922777
E-mail: books@obrien.ie; Website: www.obrien.ie
Previous edition (hardback) published 2009, reprinted 2010.

ISBN: 978-1-84717-843-5
Copyright for text © Edward J Bourke 2009

9 8 7 6 5 4 3 2 1
20 19 18 17 16

Editing, typesetting, layout and design: The O'Brien Press Ltd

Printed in Drukarnia Skleniarz, Poland.
The paper in this book is produced using pulp from managed forests
....

Edward J Bourke is a scientist who worked
at Diageo St James's Gate Global Beer Technical
Centre. He has an abiding interest in industrial
history, especially relating to Ireland, and has
published several books on shipwrecks around
the Irish coast. His links to the Guinness brewery
began at an early age as both his parents and
grandparents owned pubs in Dublin.

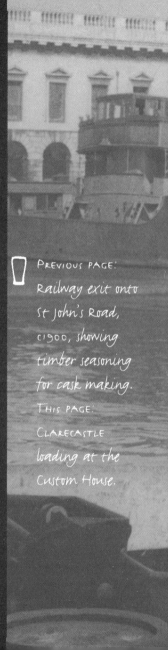

PREVIOUS PAGE:
Railway exit onto
St John's Road,
c1900, showing
timber seasoning
for cask making.
THIS PAGE:
CLARECASTLE
loading at the
Custom House.

THE
GUINNESS
STORY

THE FAMILY
THE BUSINESS
THE BLACK STUFF

EDWARD J BOURKE

THE O'BRIEN PRESS
DUBLIN

Contents

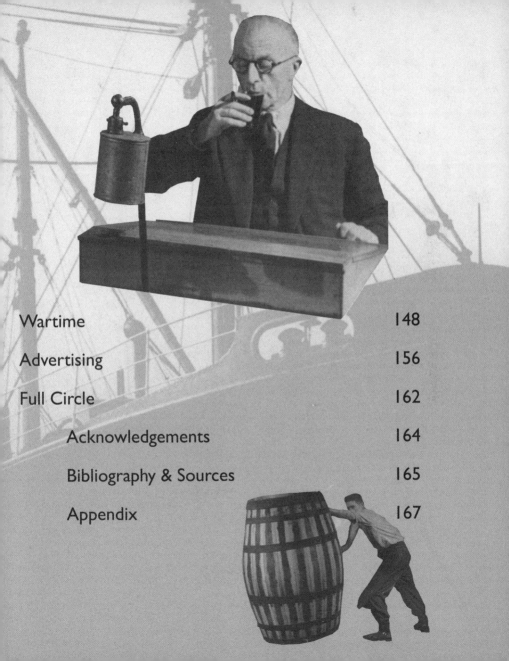

The stable yard with drays loaded for beer deliveries.

INSIDE ST JAMES'S GATE

🍺 An Overview

The Guinness Story: the Family, the Business, the Black Stuff projects an image of the pivotal role Guinness played in everyday Dublin. This is the first collection of photographs to bring to life the early days of the brewery, the Guinness dynasty, the brewing process, the unique industrial complex that grew up around St James's Gate, the day-to-day life behind the gates, the movement of Guinness beer out into the world and key moments and stories in the history of the brewery. This 250-year old story will be of interest to lovers of Guinness beer and Guinness beer memorabilia as well as those fascinated by the remarkable family of brewers and the industrial history of Ireland's most famous export, Guinness beer.

Following the purchase of the lease in 1759 by Arthur Guinness, growth of the St James's Gate brewery during the 1800s outstripped all other brewers and distillers in Ireland. This was due, in some measure, to the abundant water supply, access to the country through the Grand Canal network and, in the Victorian age, the key Guinness railway system. The skill of the brewers and the famed Guinness entrepreneurship also played vital parts in this hugely successful story of the black stuff. Before the nineteenth century ended St James's Gate had become the largest brewery in the world.

A beer export business developed that made Guinness a recognised brand all over the world. In 1936 some production for the UK moved to the newly built Park Royal brewery in London where it remained until 2005. Guinness beer went on to be brewed worldwide and is available in nearly all countries. Expansion of

By the 1960s trucks had replaced the horses.

1759   2008

Late Georgian Front Gate of the brewery, leading to the original vathouses. The keystone head is garlanded with hops.

production in Dublin during 2005 made the St James's Gate brewery amongst the largest in Europe again. From 2014 production, including the Diageo beers, moved to St James's Gate on the closure of Waterford, Kilkenny and Dundalk breweries.

During the Victorian era, the St James's Gate site developed the largest engineering works in the south of Ireland surpassed only by the Belfast shipbuilding concerns. As well as a mainline connection, a narrow-gauge railway system was built throughout the site and around the surrounding streets and quays. This had features on a scale unknown outside the Swiss mountain railways, including a spiral tunnel. The canal and river transport systems were the most extensive of their kind and became a feature of Dublin for many years. All of this illustrates how heavy industry managed transport before trucks. The fleet of brewery-owned ships were an institution at their moorings on the River Liffey at the Custom House until replaced by roll-on-roll-off transport.

Brewing took place in the largest complex of Victorian industrial buildings in Ireland. In the surrounding streets a considerable service industry occupied a vast workforce. The iron workers William Spence, grain merchants, several maltings, Richardson's horse transport and all manner of small works were nearby. They worked not just at the St James's Gate brewery but also at the other breweries and distilleries located in the area. Even the Dublin shipyard of Ross & Walpole supplied barges and pillars for buildings.

The Guinness family generated immense wealth from the business and spent their money on a series of palatial dwellings. Their interest in cruising and sailing is illustrated by their fabulous craft. The philanthropy of the family put a mark on both Dublin and England where the Iveagh Trust is the best known of their charitable works. The photographs in this book allow us an inside view of the legendary brewery, celebrating continuous industrial activity for 250 years.

The 9,000-year lease to Arthur Guinness for St James's Gate brewery, granted in 1759.

This

...Portarlington in the Kings County...
...herein after reserved and mentioned...
...these presents DOTH demise...
...late in the Possession of Sir Mar...
Nine foot and in Depth from...
...or City water Course on the North...
...Gate aforesaid late in the Posses...
...Estate of James Talbott of Temp...
...a Part of the said Malt houses...
...Advantages Emoluments apperta...
...of the premisses gratis and with...
...Guinness his Executors Administ...
...each part of the said Demised...
...Mentioned in the Schedule herein...
...of Marks Rainsford Esquire deceased...
...John Espinasse Situate on the No...

EARLY DAYS
& FAMILY
FORTUNES

Arthur Guinness

Arthur Guinness, born in 1725 at Celbridge, County Kildare, was son of Richard Guinness and Elizabeth Read. In 1722 Richard Guinness had leased a house at James Carbery's malt house and brewery, where Arthur was born in 1725. The location is now the Mucky Duck pub. Richard Guinness worked as a land steward at Oakley Park house, home of Dr Arthur Price, the then vicar of Celbridge who became Archbishop of Cashel in 1744. Both brewing and the River Liffey were part of Arthur's life from an early age.

Ten years after the death of his first wife, Elizabeth Read in 1742, Richard Guinness married Elizabeth Clare. She owned the White Hart Inn, formerly on the site of the present-day Londis Supermarket at the junction of Celbridge Main Street and the bridge over the River Liffey. There would have been brewing at the inn and no doubt the family assisted. Arthur witnessed the lease on these premises in 1749.

The Archbishop of Cashel left £100 to Arthur Guinness in his will when he died in 1752. While this is frequently quoted as the foundation of Guinness capital, there is no doubt that the Guinness family was comfortable. The family lived at Viney House in Celbridge between 1752 and 1764, by which time Arthur and his brother Richard had moved to Leixlip where Arthur leased a brewery in 1755 from George Bryams on the site of the modern Courtyard Hotel. A copy of the lease, bearing Arthur's signature, is on display in the hotel. The two Guinness brothers supplied beer from their Leixlip brewery to the Castletown estate which employed some 300

Portrait of Arthur Guinness.

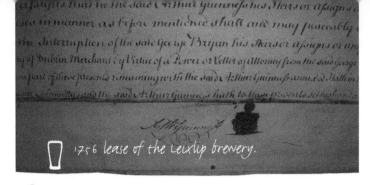

1756 lease of the Leixlip brewery.

men. Local folklore claims that the Castletown beer was black, but this seems unlikely as ale alone was brewed in St James's Gate from 1759 to the late 1770s.

Arthur left the Leixlip brewery in charge of his brother Richard when he moved to Dublin at the end of 1759. The family had several relations already well established in business in Dublin and Arthur's connections were considerable. By 1761 he had married Olivia Whitmore, a well-born young lady, whose mother was a Grattan and

may have been related to Henry Grattan, the parliamentarian. The marriage took place in St Mary's Church at the Junction of Jervis Street and Mary Street. She brought a dowry of £1,000 – a very substantial amount at the time. Arthur was elected Warden of the Corporation of Brewers in 1763 and the following year he was living in Beaumont in considerable style.

It is not clear when the first brewery was established at St James's Gate, but in 1670 Giles Mee, a city alderman, obtained water rights in the parish and these, along with the brewery, were transferred to his son-in-law Sir Mark Rainsford. By 1693 Alderman Mark Rainsford was recorded as a brewer at St James's Gate. When he died in 1709 his son took over but ceased business in November 1715, selling a 100-year lease to Paul Espinasse. Captain Espinasse died in a fall from a horse near Drogheda in 1750 and the brewery was disused for a period and advertised for sale in 1750, 1753 and again in 1754 before Mark Rainsford junior sold the lease to

LEFT: Site of the Guinness brothers' brewery at Leixlip in 1756, now the Courtyard Hotel.

RIGHT: Memorial in St James's Church to Mark Rainsford (also spelt Ransford), former owner of St James's Gate brewery.

Oakley Park, Celbridge, County Kildare, where Arthur's father was steward to Dr Arthur Price, later Archbishop of Cashel.

Arthur Guinness's admission to the Guild of Dublin Brewers.

Arthur Guinness on the last day of December 1759.

The Corporation of Brewers of Dublin was established by royal charter of King William in 1696. It regulated the brewing trade in Dublin. Their minutes of Tuesday, 24 April 1759 in the Guinness archive record:

A meeting of the master and wardens of brethren of this Corporation pursuant to due notice given, the petition of Arthur Guinness being read praying to be admitted to the franchises and liberties of this corporation he was accordingly admitted paying a fine of two guineas ...

Those present at the meeting were James Taylor, master; Epp Thwaites, warden; Hugh Trevor and John Forster. These brewers were prominent among the Freemen of Dublin, and seven of their family names appear on the roll of Mayors of Dublin in the eighteenth century. Arthur did not have to suffer an apprenticeship as his previous experience as a brewer was taken into account. The social standing of the Guinness family grew down through the generations. Benjamin Guinness, Arthur's grandson, became Lord Mayor of Dublin in 1851. From the 1880s the role of the Guinness family in community life was recognised and three peerages were

Early on, Arthur Guinness was a man of means as evidenced by these investmen properties, still standing in Leixlip today.

established: Ardilaun, Iveagh and Moyne, for the Guinness family.

The founding father, Arthur Guinness, died at a house on Mountjoy Square in 1803 and his wife also died there in 1814. Some sources believe it to be number 68 Mountjoy Square, while his son, William Lunell Guinness, lived at 19 on the corner of Belvedere Place. The exact house is not positively identified. Arthur Guinness was buried in a vault at Oughterard churchyard near Sallins, County Kildare. The round tower is just visible from the M7 motorway. This was the family burial place of the Reads – his mother's relations. His Read cousins were cutlers in Parliament Street.

A Brewers' City

Competition in the Dublin beer trade was intense with thirty-five

4 Parliament Street, once Read cutlers'
shop, which claimed to be the oldest in
Dublin. Arthur's mother, Elizabeth, was a
member of the Read family.

breweries listed in the Watson's Dublin trade directory. Arthur Guinness was not the only brewer in the immediate area; there was also a Thomas Greene brewing at St James's Gate in the early years. A further five brewers operated in James's Street and Thomas Street. In later years even more brewers occupied the district, taking advantage of the main city water supply passing down the street. There was also a ready market because in 1798, fifty-two of the 190 houses in James's Street were licensed premises.

Arthur Guinness is buried at Oughterard in Kildare, in the shadow of a twelfth-century round tower.

Porter

Porter became popular from 1722 in London, especially among the porters at Covent Garden market, from which the name is thought to originate. Imports of porter into Ireland expanded rapidly until between 1762 and 1773, the quantity had increased from 28,000 barrels to 58,000 barrels. Evidence was given to the Irish Parliament on 10 November 1773 by several Dublin brewers. Mr Thwaites, the Master of the Corporation, said that the number of brewers had dropped from seventy to thirty and that none had made a profit for seven years. The porter import trade was influenced by a disparity in excise duty with five shillings and sixpence duty per barrel paid on Irish porter. English porter had a net duty of three pence per barrel because there was an export bounty of a shilling recoverable on the English duty of fifteen pence per barrel. At this time Arthur had

Pyramids of wooden casks in the cooperage yard had to be hosed with water in warm weather to prevent drying out.

threatened to move production to Holyhead or Carnavon, to avail of the lower English duty. He visited Wales and said that if he believed the excise situation would continue another seven years that he would move there. The Parliament's response was to close the loophole on imports by applying an extra duty on imported beer, but relief was given in 1777. It is believed that the next year, in 1778, porter brewing commenced at the St James's Gate brewery. By 1816 the import trade was reversed and 1,000 barrels of porter were being exported to England annually.

Water Fight

In 1775 a Dublin Corporation committee and sheriff had attempted to cut off and fill in the water course from which the brewery drew its free water supplies. The right to water had been granted to a previous owner, Giles Mee, but arguably the period had expired. Arthur defended his water by threatening the party with a pickaxe. This action highlighted the general shortage of water in Dublin. The matter was not pursued probably because the Grand Canal had been under construction since 1757 and the first section was nearing completion. The supply of Grand Canal water to the City Basin commenced in 1776 and alleviated the general shortage of water in Dublin. Hitherto the Dodder River was diverted to the City watercourse at Templeogue and then into the Poddle filling the City Basin. The Canal was completed in stages to 1800 and opened up transport to the midlands of Ireland for the conveyance of malt and barley and export of beer.

Flour Riot

In the 1790s there was extreme poverty in the narrow streets around the brewery. In 1789 the French Revolution broke out over the price and scarcity of flour. In Dublin a fragile peace was maintained by magistrates, freemen and ultimately troops. The barracks opposite the brewery would have been within hailing distance. This is an extract of a letter from Dublin written on 6 June 1793, published in *Lloyds Evening Post*:

A numerous mob, from the Earl of Meath's estate, appeared in the streets on Monday evening, and plundered several houses of butter, bread, bacon and cheese. ... It is to be observed that the equally unfortunate people from whom they plunder are not in a much better situation than they are themselves.

Farmers are afraid to send their goods in consequence ... Three car loads of flour were stopped yesterday by a banditi from the Liberty parts and ... several of the bags were emptied in the streets principally in Thomas Court and Rainsford Street. The lower females in these quarters carried their contents off in their aprons. Mr Guinness and two or three other gentlemen, armed, together with a few soldiers, immediately proceeded after the depredators and were soon joined by a larger party of the army, horse and foot accompanied by some magistrates when a search commenced of many suspected houses in the course of which, a few bags were recovered, of fifteen carried off, and several small quantities in aprons, quilts, boxes cradles etc. A few persons, men and women were arrested and conveyed to prison.

Arthur Guinness and Emancipation

In 1813 there was agitation for Catholic Emancipation and repeal of the Penal Laws led by Daniel O'Connell. Members of the licensed trade were approached and even attacked for selling Guinness beer. Later Daniel O'Connell's son established a brewery and sold O'Connell's ale. The Guinness family refuted the allegation of their opposition to Emancipation in the *Freeman's Journal* of 17 May 1813:

> A most false and slanderous report has been circulated for some time past, that we had signed a petition to Parliament against the claims of our Catholic Brethren ... we now feel ourselves called upon to declare as follows:

> That we did not sign that, or any petition against the claims of our Catholic countrymen, and that the petition is in nature in direct opposition to our sentiments and principles ... That so far from having signed the anti Catholic Petition, we heartily and cordially joined in and signed the petition to Parliament for the complete emancipation of our Catholic brethren ... We are authorised further to appeal to our long established and well known principles of brotherly love towards our Catholic fellow subjects, which principles we derived from our father, who was also the early and unshaken friend of the Catholics of Ireland ... Now we do hereby offer a reward of five hundred pounds to any person or persons, who shall ... discover and prosecute to conviction the person or persons who ... have invented and circulated this base and unfounded report, and have thus illegally and invidiously attempted to injure our character and property.

> *Arthur, Benjamin and William L. Guinness*

Fortunes of the Brewery

Better financial circumstances during the Napoleonic wars (1800–15) led to greater prosperity. Water supply, transport and investment capital benefitted the brewery at St James's Gate. The quantity of ale brewed decreased steadily and ceased altogether in 1799. Porter brewing commenced from the late 1770s and by 1800 the annual output was 10,000 barrels. In 1801 West Indies Porter, a precursor to modern-day Foreign Extra Stout, was first brewed. Stout was an adjective used to qualify porter from the 1820s and the term extra stout porter was applied to a stronger and more robust version of porter itself.

Loading exports at Liverpool.

Output doubled between 1801 and 1802 and doubled again by 1808 but collapsed at the end of the Napoleonic wars. Export to Liverpool and Bristol was managed by agents G&S Lunell and shippers Samuel Waring. At this time the English canal system became a distribution route for exports. Another agent, Sparks Moline, commenced distribution in London. Growth in the 1830s was steady and soon the 1809 peak was achieved and surpassed.

Production at the St James's Gate brewery exceeded that of Beamish in Cork by 1838, making St James's Gate brewery the largest in Ireland. In the early days there were two larger breweries in Dublin and more beer was exported from Cork than Dublin. There was a 20% increase in 1845, possibly due to an influx of people into Dublin at the start of the Great Famine. St James's Gate produced just over 100,000 barrels in 1846. Guinness remained small compared with the major London breweries as late as the 1850s. By 1860 output had doubled again. The big bottling and ships' stores concerns became prominent customers for Guinness. These were E&J Burke at Atlas Street and McFee in Norfolk Street in Liverpool. There were also Manns and Hills at Southampton and Poussay in Paris. In 1881 production exceeded a million barrels (1.6 million hectolitres).

By 1914 St James's Gate was the largest brewery in the world and a site was acquired to build a brewery at Trafford Park, Manchester. Grain scarcity, a compulsory alcohol reduction and the alcohol taxation imposed during the First World War interrupted growth. When adjusted to a standard gravity strength the 1914 output amounted to 2.45 million barrels and that in 1918 was only 0.92 million barrels. The excise duty had increased from seven shillings and nine pence per barrel to a hundred shillings. At the end of the war the maximum permitted gravity for England was 1032 and Ireland 1047. This compared with pre-war strength of 1073 for Extra Stout and 1058 for porter. Production growth resumed and reached 3 million barrels (4.8 million hectolitres) by 1920.

Politics and Production in London

The 1920s were a period of depression and political instability in Ireland as the new state became established. Plans were developed for

Park Royal brewery, in London, was opened in 1936.

a new brewery at Park Royal, London, to supply the south of England trade. On completion in 1936, it took on a substantial share of the British trade.

The Labour government in Britain fell in 1931 at a time of great economic crisis. The government in Ireland also changed from Cumann na Gael to Fianna Fáil in the 1932 general election. Because of the economic state of the country the Taoiseach, Eamon de Valera, renounced the payment of land annuities to Britain. These were repayments of mortgages on farms sold under the Gladstone, Ashbourne, Chichester and Wyndham land acts which allowed tenants buy out their rented farms from landlords. There commenced a period known as the 'economic war'. Both sides imposed penal duties and self-sufficiency was promoted in Ireland.

In 1932 JH Thomas, the UK Secretary of State, met with Lord Iveagh of the Guinness company. At the meeting, due to the economic war over the renunciation of the land annuities, a threat was made that if a brewery was not established in Britain the UK

Lagos brewery, opened in 1960.

Barrels and transportable tanks await loading onto the LADY PATRICIA at City Quay.

government would introduce extra duty on beer from Ireland. There had been rumours in the Dublin papers suggesting that the pre-First World War Manchester brewery project was being reassessed. The result was immediate secret action to acquire land near London and construction of Park Royal brewery commenced without delay. Experiments had already been conducted which indicated that the Dublin water was not essential to the quality of Guinness beer as was widely believed and that quality would not be affected.

Export

Export of beers built up from the late 1940s carried by traders down the west coast of Africa and to the Caribbean. This trade lead to another peak in production at St James's Gate in 1959. Export volume had increased dramatically from 25,000 barrels in 1948 to 90,000 in 1951, 140,000 in 1955, 300,000 in 1964 and 500,000 in 1970. After demand reached 286,000 barrels for Nigeria in 1961, local brewing commenced at Lagos in 1963. Production in Cameroon, Ghana, Indonesia, Malaya, Jamaica and Kenya along with further contract production followed subsequently. This reduced volume brewed at St James's Gate to about 4.5 million hectolitres where it remained until 2005. Then capacity was increased to 6.5 million hectolitres when the whole UK production returned to St James's Gate on the closure of the Park Royal brewery.

Floating the Company

In 1886 Edward Cecil Guinness floated the brewery on the London

Stock Exchange. His primary motivation was to relieve himself of the burden of managing the company as a sole proprietor. Edward Baring, who became Lord Revelstoke in 1885, undervalued the company and a favoured few took up the bulk of the issue. His firm Barings Bank received a million of the four million shares on offer and other banks took a further 1.2 million. Family and management were allocated small holdings. Lord Ardilaun £15,000, Claude £3,000, Reginald £2,000; John Tertius Purser refused £5,000, because the new Barings selected director Herman Hoskier received £6,000. The public keenly snapped up the remainder. There was outrage in the markets and it was felt that the banks had behaved very badly. Then Sir Edward used the fortune of £950,000 he had received from the company as dividends in the six years before flotation to increase his holding of 33% of the company to buy a controlling interest in only two years. There was much adverse comment in the financial press about the allocation of the shares. The market disquiet was later mirrored in the corporate battle when Distillers Company was taken over in 1987.

Competition within the Family

The first Arthur's daughter, Elizabeth Guinness, 1763–1847, married Frederick Darley. In 1814 Darley's brewery in Stillorgan, County Dublin, traded as Darley and Guinness. Darley's had breweries in Bray and Great Britain Street as well. The Darley cousins continued in business until 1937 at a brewery in Ardee Street even being granted a 'change of yeast' from St James's Gate in the 1890s.

In 1838 John Grattan Guinness junior had been sacked from the brewery business in Dublin, started by his grandfather, for drunkenness and 'mixing with degraded society'. His uncle, the second Arthur Guinness, bought him a brewery in Bristol to try to give him another chance. This was the first attempt by the company to establish brewing in Britain and exploit the growing market established by the agents. Unfortunately John Grattan Guinness does not seem to have been a businessman, and the Bristol brewery went under in 1845. Much later, after he fell into poverty, John Grattan tried ungratefully and unsuccessfully to sue his cousin Benjamin Guinness for wrongful dismissal from the Dublin brewery.

The original brewery at Leixlip established in 1755 continued under the management of Richard Guinness until 1803. Another intriguing reference is mentioned in a letter by a Mr Brophy to the *Evening Telegraph* on 24 April 1891:

> I have before me an old book in which the author describing Carlow in 1814 states: 'The River Greene turns two mills of importance erected by Mr Greene beside which he has also a brewery in the town of Carlow under the direction of Mr Guinness, a scientific brewer, from the metropolis.'

Even Lord Iveagh established a micro brewery at Elveden Estate, brewing Elveden stout in 2004.

Coopers charred the wooden casks to clean them and impart some flavour to the beer.

MAKING THE GUINNESS BEER

ABOVE: Barley provides the sugar.
RIGHT: Hops provide flavour and
keep the beer from spoilage.
OPPOSITE TOP: Malt, made from
barley, makes the sugars available
for yeast. Some of the barley is
roasted for colour and flavour.

The Ingredients & the Process

The infamous 'pint of plain' is brewed from four main ingredients:
malted barley, hops, water and brewer's yeast.

Barley grows in temperate climates and is the main
ingredient in beer made in Europe, North America
and the equivalent latitudes in the southern
hemisphere. Barley can be sown in winter or
spring for harvest in early autumn. The second
main ingredient is hops that grow in similar
latitudes. Hops grow as vines, supported on a network
of poles and wires. Hops are added to prevent spoilage; the
resin squeezed from the hop flower cones contains a flavoursome
natural antibacterial substance and gives beer its character.

*Traditional malting – the men used wooden shovels
and worked barefoot, so as not to damage the malt.*

Beer is made by taking barley and allowing it to sprout under controlled conditions in the malting process. Formerly barley was spread over vast wooden floors and the grain was turned by hand and sprayed with water, allowing it to germinate as if it was about to grow in the soil. Today the barley is processed in concrete drums and handled mechanically. The brief growth of the barley softens the grain and produces the enzymes to digest the starch. Heating in a kiln halts growth abruptly. Dried malt can be stored and later milled into coarse flour just before brewing. The milled malt, including the grain husks, is then mashed into hot water.

Pure water in vast quantity is a vital ingredient in production of beer. Extracted from the River Liffey high in the Wicklow hills, the water comes in to St James's Gate brewery from the Dublin city waterworks at Poulaphuca. The mash is held warm for a period, during which time enzymes in the malt convert the starch to sugar. This porridge-like mash is spread onto the floor of a kieve or lauter tun or sometimes a mash filter and the sugary solution called wort is filtered from the husks of the barley. Some roasted barley is added for colour. The wort is boiled vigorously to evaporate grainy flavours and hops are added for flavour and preservation. Then, after cooling, the wort is transferred with addition of yeast to fermentation vessels.

This is where the production of whisky and beer differ, as the wort for beer is clear liquor with hops, while the fermentation substrate for whiskey has all the grain included and no hops. The yeast converts the sugar to alcohol and carbon dioxide, developing

Digging out a hop back was hot and thirsty work, as the hops are separated from the boiling worts.

the full flavour of the beer. During fermentation the yeast replicates and produces 12 tonnes of alcohol and a similar amount of carbon dioxide from the sugars while turning 2,000 hectolitres of wort into Guinness. After a period of maturation, the beer is filled into kegs for delivery to bars or transported by tanker to a bottling or canning plant. Distribution is a vital part of the process and Guinness has to be at the forefront of logistics to achieve worldwide impact in sales.

Wooden vats stored millions of pints while the beer matured.
BELOW: Installing one of the cylindrical vessels which contain 4,000 hectolitres or half a million pints.

The Beers

The products brewed at St James's Gate brewery are Draught Stout, Extra Stout, known as Original in the UK, Foreign Extra Stout and Special Export at 8% alcohol specially for Belgium. In the 1960s Guinness renewed their interest in the ale business through the association with, and eventual acquisition of, Smithwick's brewery in Kilkenny, Macardle's in Dundalk, Perry's in Rathdowney and Cherry's in Waterford. Phoenix Ale was brewed at St James's Gate initially and later Smithwick's ale and Kilkenny ale. Furstenberg lager was brewed at St James's Gate between 1987 and 1991. Guinness bought the Great Northern Brewery in Dundalk in 1959 and commenced brewing Harp lager, which is brewed today at St James's Gate, along with all the company ales and lagers. Harp itself became a successful brand and was brewed and distributed by a consortium of brewers. By 1976 sales reached 2.2 million barrels, but it declined as other lagers were adopted by the trade.

The modern brewhouse has stainless steel vessels, heated by steam.

Wort was boiled in coal-fired coppers, to bring out the flavour of hops.

Invention of Nitrogenated Draught Stout

Beer was always carbonated because of the fermentation by yeast but the smooth creamy head of Guinness beer (Guinness beer traditionally has a head not just foam) is partly due to nitrogen dissolved in the beer. The dispense system using pumps from a vented barrel allowed air into contact with the beer. One story tells that pubs near the brewery in the centre of Dublin were served by horse and cart and the rattling of the barrels over cobblestones whipped in extra air from the headspace. This gave these local pubs a superior pint and the work of inventive brewer Sammy Hildebrand developed this observation in the 1960s to deliver the nitrogenated beer that we know today. Whatever the veracity of the yarn, it is a good story. (Sammy did not just develop draught Guinness beer. He also built a submarine at home and his two sons piloted it underwater in a lock on the Grand Canal in the 1960s.)

The Widget

The distinctive creamy head of draught Guinness beer was replicated in can and bottle by the invention of the widget which releases nitrogen when pressure is released to form bubbles in the liquid, knocking more dissolved nitrogen out of the solution to form the creamy head on the beer.

Londoners migrated to the south of England hop farms for the picking, c1900.

45

Checking the roast.

From Farm to Tap

The brewery has always been active in the selection and breeding of malting barley. An experimental programme to examine and select improved varieties was conducted at the brewery between 1900 and 1990. This involved testing vast numbers of barley samples from trial plots. The work determined the malting and brewing quality of the barley. Meanwhile agronomists observed the yield per acre, sturdiness of straw which gave resistance to lodging and disease resistance. There would follow full scale trials in the field and brewery.

ES Beaven (1857–1941) was one of the leading breeders of barley in the first half of the twentieth century. He was a maltster in Warminster, Wiltshire, and he began to make experimental trials of barley. One outcome of his experiments was a new variety, Plumage-Archer, which was one of the principal types of malting barleys until new hybrids, such as Proctor, were introduced after the Second World War. Much of Beaven's work was published posthumously in the book *Barley* (1947).

Both the maltings and the experimental station were taken over by the brewery. One of the most suitable varieties discovered by the Irish side of the breeding programme was Spratt-Archer – a cross between Danish and Irish barley which yielded a resistant sturdy variety, ideally suited to Irish growing conditions. It lasted twenty years in agricultural use. A barley research station at Ballinacurra in Cork was supported for many years. More modern higher yielding varieties barely survive five years before they succumb to disease or are surpassed. Just prior to the harvest a barley tour would visit growers to assess the harvest both in quantity and quality. The excursion took the form of a picnic at several sites and was an opportunity to meet growers, malsters and traders socially. There were maltings at St James's Gate to supply about half of the malt used. Immense storage bins at Robert Street were filled with grain at harvest. The kilns of the malting plant were used as driers to remove moisture and preserve the grain.

This grain would be malted as required for the rest of the year. Similar quantities of barley were taken in to the flaking plant for rolling into flakes or roasting.

All this activity is now separated from the brewing operations and has become the responsibility of the maltster. Every year just before Christmas the final of the malting barley competition takes place at the brewery. The winning entries from each region go forward for finals to win a hotly contested cup for the finest malting barley in Ireland.

Hop pockets (sacks) stacked in a cool warehouse, situated over giant water reservoirs, during the 1940s.

In 1880 a malt store was constructed at Robert Street with honeycomb silos built of brick and emptied by trains. It still remains in use.

THE BREWERY
BUILDINGS

St James's Gate, which describes the location of the brewery, was an ancient entrance to the city of Dublin. It was a suitable location for industry as the main route for the corn supply into Dublin passed through the gate. The city water supply from the River Poddle also passed through the area en route in to the city. St James's Gate appears on Speed's map of Dublin in 1610 and Brooking's map of 1728. St James's Gate was so named because it was the traditional departure point for pilgrims en route from Dublin to the shrine of St James at Santiago de Compostella in Spain. It appears that the travellers boarded boats on the River Liffey and were taken to larger ships downriver. The local parish is that of St James's. The original St James's Gate, which formed part of the city walls, was demolished in 1734 by Paul Espinasse, a former owner of the brewery.

The St James's Gate site, which Arthur Guinness acquired in 1759, was a very modest affair, consisting of four acres (just over 2.5 hectares) of land, containing a copper, a kieve (a mash tun), a mill, two malthouses, stabling for twelve horses and a loft to hold 200 tons of hay. The size of the operation remained small into the 1820s, reflecting the brewery output.

From 1880 to 1975, kieves originally built by Spence of Dublin, were used to separate the wort from the grain.

ABOVE: View of St James's Gate brewery.

RIGHT: A pencil sketch by Harry Kernoff (1900–74), dated 1928, depicts the brewery from the esplanade opposite Victoria Quay. While the DWD windmill is prominent, none of the other buildings exist today.

Victorian Glory

The rapid expansion in trade through the 1850s brought a spate of building and mechanisation. The complex of Victorian buildings that survive today date from expansion in 1870 and especially after the business became a public company in 1886. A policy of property acquisition secured sites to bring the whole complex to 68 acres (44.5 hectares) at its peak. The largest acquisition was the Dublin Whiskey Distillery buildings, including the windmill purchased in the late 1940s and disposed of to the Digital Hub along with four vat houses and the hop store in 2002. There was modernisation in the 1950s and again in the 1980s.

The most prominent structures are the Robert Street malt store, the Market Street Storehouse and the flaking plant. These dominate the skyline in the area, being tall buildings located at a height of 100 feet (30.5 metres) above the Liffey bank. The earlier buildings on the site include the two vat houses marked on the original site map. The northern half of the site or Lower Level was acquired from 1850 and originally comprised two streets of small industries including several tanneries, three smaller breweries, and a malt-roasting plant. The Guinness brewery was the largest concern in a whole district that included, at various times, twelve distilleries and twenty breweries with their associated maltings. Engineering works like Spence and numerous service industries supported the brewing operation.

LEFT: In 1895, a pedestrian tunnel was built beside the railway tunnel designed by James Greathead, who built many of the London Underground tunnels.

ABOVE: The site was served by an extensive narrow-gauge railway system from 1880 to 1960.

Guinness Storehouse

Fermentation occurred from 1903 to 1988 in the Market Street storehouse – now the Guinness Storehouse Visitors' Centre. This vast steel-framed, brick-clad building was designed by the engineering department in 1901 and commenced construction in 1903. The steelwork consisted of giant girders made by Sir William Arol, who is best known for the construction of the Forth railway bridge. At the time it was impossible to roll single girders of the required size, so the storehouse giant girders were constructed by riveting together standard smaller sections – in total 3,600 tons of steel were used. The overall design was after the Chicago school of architecture with steel support and curtain walls, a technique used on the early New York skyscrapers.

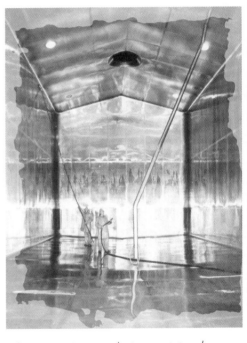

☐ The giant 26M tun – a fermentation vessel situated in the storehouse – held 12,000 hectolitres or a million and a half pints and was the largest beer fermentation vessel in the world.

Fermentation

The brewery achieved economies of scale where others merely duplicated equipment. An example was tun number 26M situated in the Storehouse. It was the largest beer fermentation vessel in the world. It contained 8,000 barrels, or 12,000 hectolitres of foaming fermenting beer. It took twenty-four hours to fill and two rotating propellers turned continuously to break the foam that arose from the fermentation. During the twenty-four hours it took to fill, the fermentation commenced. Then there was a race against time to complete filling and measure the volume for excise payment before the rich creamy foam would pour out the doorway enveloping the floor. It was barely filled when it was time to start emptying. It had some characteristics of a continuous fermentation operation. The vessels were kept in pristine condition by manual washing and scrubbing with brushes on a 30-foot (9-metre) pole. Men entered the vessels only after they had seen a candle placed on the floor burn strongly to indicate that none of the deadly carbon dioxide remained in the atmosphere. Modern beer vessels are individually insulated and clad, removing the need for surrounding buildings. Set in a three-foot thick concrete entablature, each maturation vessel weighs 350 tons when full. They contain the equivalent of a million pints of beer.

Maltings

Much of the activity that formerly occurred on the brewery site

ABOVE: The Plunketts moved the maltings to Islandbridge and took the name Belview with them. Today the building houses apartments.

INSET: Plunkett's Belview maltings, to the rear of the brewery, supplied St James's Gate with malt and roast barley.

OPPOSITE: Rows of narrow-gauge railway wagons await loading at Cooks Lane maltings, demolished to make way for the fermentation plant.

has moved to supplier locations. The Plunkett family of malsters claimed the invention of roast malt and had a roast-house to the rear of the brewery at Belview. The maltings at Belview became part of the brewery site and the Plunketts built another maltings at Islandbridge, also called Belview, which supplied the brewery to the 1980s. There were brewery maltings at Cooks Lane and also Robert Street, but all malt comes in to the site from devoted malt suppliers nowadays.

The Hibernian Mills

Arthur Guinness built a flour mill in 1782 and at one stage it accounted for a quarter of his profits. Wilson's Directory describes his business as brewer and flour miller between 1793 and 1807. On the 14 June 1806 the Freeman's Journal reported:

A most alarming fire broke out yesterday morning at two o'clock

in the malt mill erected on the rising ground beyond Kilmainham belonging to Messrs Guinness. It raged with such ferocity and violence that all endeavours to check or extinguish it proved ineffective till the whole of the spacious building was consumed. Several hundred barrels of flour and malt were destroyed. We regret to mention that the loss on this occasion must have been considerable as only part of the concerns were insured.

Two days later Globe Insurance advertised that their fire engine (superior to any in the city) had attended. They mentioned that insurance was a prudent business measure to alleviate crippling losses. The Guinness company had the last word, however, in an advertisement in the paper of 28 July 1806 thanking Hibernian Insurance for the settlement of their portion of the damages claim, amounting to £4,750 associated with the fire at their mill.

The flour business survived until about 1815. Arthur Guinness was a director of Hibernian Insurance. His son William Lunell became a director of Norwich Union Insurance. Their particular attention to insurance may have resulted from a fire during the early days of the brewery. On the night of 26 December 1765 a fire broke out in a small back house at the brewery. The water supply was abundant and the flames were rapidly suppressed.

Guinness Power Station

Unusually, the site contains a large power station. Combined heat and power is much advocated as a fuel-efficient energy system, but Guinness was among the early adopters of this system with

The Art Deco-style, brick-clad power station supplied steam and electricity from 1949 until it was replaced by gas turbines in 2000.

the power station built in 1947 on the site of the Phoenix or Madder's brewery, previously owned by Daniel O'Connell junior, and closed in 1913. O'Connell's ale was made subsequently by Darcy's and then Watkins, Jameson and Pim, in nearby Ardee Street, until 1939.

Cask-racking shed.

BREWERY LIFE

 ## City within a City

The brewery was like a city within itself and at its peak in about 1960 had nearly 5,000 permanent workers and several hundred contractors hired in from McLoughlin & Harvey. Many customs and practices, as well as petty regulations, governed day-to-day life.

The site was divided into upper and lower levels separated by James's Street and linked by three tunnels. The gentlemen brewers ruled the Upper Level and considered that transport and utilities situated in the Lower Level were inferior.

One prospective worker was asked about his previous employment and mentioned that he had been in the Guards. His interviewer thought he had found a kindred spirit and asked what regiment and whether he had served overseas. The interviewer could barely conceal his disappointment on learning that the interviewee meant An Garda Síochána (the Irish police).

The nine dining areas maintained a strict formality and separation between staff grades.

Luncheon

Lunch was a high point in the brewery day. The starched white tablecloths and waitress service in the staff dining room contrasted with the self-service for the men. Staff would be reminded by a stern head waiter that jackets were worn at luncheon if they dared to come incorrectly attired or indeed remove their jackets while eating. There were daunting protocols with set tables and places arranged by invitation where the same six people lunched together at the same time for perhaps their entire brewery career. Mixing of different grades of staff did not seem to occur. A bottle of ale, stout or lager was at each place carefully selected according to the taste of each regular diner. Alternatively a soft drink was there for the non-drinkers. The female staff rarely sat at the same table as the men as impolite conversation or lewd tales could offend.

There were at least nine different dining rooms on the site for directors down to apprentices. The medical people dined in splendid isolation in the medical centre. The traffic men ate at a canteen known as the 'Taj Mahal', from whence they issued forth on their deliveries after a hearty breakfast. In addition to this, baskets of food were distributed to mess rooms in the production areas so that a breakfast, or supper, could be cooked outside of serving times.

Business was not discussed until coffee when a series of informal meetings arranged all necessary items of brewery business. At Park Royal brewery a few hands of bridge were normally played over coffee.

Spillage

Spillage was a serious matter and all pipelines were accessed through locked valves and stopcocks. The beer route would be made by the operators, checked by the foreman and then authorised after further checking by a staff man or clerk. On one occasion a significant spillage occurred and the clerk sought to cover up the damage by taking a little from each of the other vats so that the loss was not apparent. His subterfuge was discovered and he was dismissed.

When beer was being transferred manually from one vat to another as part of a blend the level would be called out by a man observing the beer from the hatchway at the top of the vessel. One dark night the man in question was Christy. He was working in dim light and the surface of the beer was particularly still and reflective. The manway door at the bottom of the vessel came into sight as the level dropped and in the dimly lit circumstances he observed the reflection of the bottom of the door on the surface of the beer. Since he could see the bottom of the door he called the vessel empty and the next stage was to open the door and commence cleaning. Unfortunately there was about three feet of beer remaining to reflect the mirage of the door bottom and this gushed out in a tidal wave when the door was opened.

A similar routing error during a strike in 1974 could have been more serious if the last vat containing yeast had been lost. No beer was being produced but the yeast had to be kept alive. Four vats of gyle (unfermented wort), containing a high level of yeast were kept cold to avoid fermenting the beer and preserve the irreplaceable yeast. The vats were circulated through a cooler to maintain a low temperature. The route was made manually by opening a series of valves and all appeared to proceed correctly. On the next shift an attempt was made to take a sample and to the horror of all, the vat was empty. It had been transferred completely to another warm vessel and had fermented. The yeast was exhausted and disaster only averted by a narrow margin because another small gyle vessel survived.

Stoking coal-burning boilers about 1900.

Hot Work

Much of the brewhouse work was done as quickly as possible even before the vessels had cooled. This ensured minimum vessel turnaround time. Extra liquid refreshment encouraged such work thus as ordained in a board order.

> No extra beer allowance will be given for work done in circumstances that are merely more uncomfortable than normal. However an extra allowance of one pint bottle will be given during each four hours of actual or standard duty, for work done in all enclosed vessels which are at a very high temperature, and in addition kieves and hopbacks from which hot brewing materials are handled manually.

Large bottles of lemonade were available ad lib on the kieve stage and several dozen were delivered there each morning. Most of the hot work was done wearing a minimum of clothing and when secretaries (female) approached the area the warning cry would go out, 'ladies on the floor'.

The Tap

Brewery men were entitled to two pints daily at the tap. It was normal to have a

Men received two pints daily as a beer allowance, served at taps around the site.

beer break as others might have a tea break. There were taps at the back gate and at the cooperage. Each man had a key with his number for clocking in and this recorded beer issue as well. In addition, a staff man had a book of dockets and any man who worked well was given a docket as reward. Misappropriation or forging of dockets was treated severely. One man did a private job on a boat for a staff man who gave him a docket for a single pint – the docket was altered to four pints. When this was detected the man was fired on the spot.

In the 1970s one of the directors, Lord Boyd, was staying with his family at the brewery dwelling at 98 James Street. He thought that he would visit the night workers and he went around and spoke with those on night duty. They mentioned that he might like to visit the tap but would have to sign a docket for beer. However, he neglected to state the amount of beer on the docket so it was pinned to the wall for all to draw a pint. This became known as the long docket and was much appreciated by all the men.

Then there was a raffle; tickets cost two pence and a further pint was free with each ticket – nobody was clear what the prize was. If a man opted not to receive beer, he was entitled to five shillings scrip money monthly. Many teetotallers availed of this option.

Revising the Beer Allowance

The men's beer allowance was changed from draught to bottle on 1 February 1972 and the taps then existing at the back gate, container and traffic departments were closed. The change in arrangements was announced thus:

A beer break at the tap.

Bottled beer is issued from two depots which are controlled by the Administrative services section of the general services department. Heads of departments are responsible for ensuring that there are no abuses in the consumption of beer in the areas under their control. The cash allowance in lieu of beer allowance is £0.125 or 12½p per week and the allowance in lieu of a single pint will be calculated at the rate of 1.25p per pint. The weekly total will be rounded up to the next 1p.

Each batch of beer produced was tasted formally by a trained panel.

This was an early encouragement in the direction of responsible drinking. The pint bottles were issued unlabelled and though they contained just the normal bottle-conditioned Guinness they were highly prized as a gift because the public were convinced that they contained a very special recipe. In more recent times each employee has an allowance of Diageo products available through the bottle shop on site, subject of course to taxation as benefit-in-kind.

The Daily Ritual of Tasting the Beer

Daily at the brewery, beer is tasted formally in controlled conditions so that its quality and consistency can be assessed. Despite all modern analytical techniques, tasting is the final arbiter of quality. Strict marking schemes and statistical analysis of the data are applied.

First-class Brewers

At the turn of the nineteenth century, graduates of Trinity College Dublin were told that but for the Boer War they would have had no chance of getting jobs in the brewery. William Sealy Gossett joined the brewery in 1899 as a junior brewer with a first-class degree in Mathematics. Just a few years before, in 1893, the brewery had established a chemists' laboratory led by TB Case who had a first-class chemistry degree from Oxford. This established the tradition that brewers had first-class degrees from either Oxford or Cambridge. At that time an experimental brewery had been built to test the suitability of various malts for brewing. Since the experiments were extensive, involving taking a trial plot of barley through malting and then brewing, the number of replications of the test was limited. This drew in to question the reliability of the result obtained. In 1906 Gossett took a sabbatical year as was the custom at that time. He went to study under Karl Pearson in London. The fruit of his labour was a mathematical test of significance of experimental data. It was published in 1908 in *Biometrika*, and became known as 'Student's T-test'. He apparently was not encouraged to publish under his own name and used the pseudonym 'Student'. No correspondence survives on this topic, but it is probable that his superiors were jealous of his significant achievement. He became head brewer at the newly opened Park Royal brewery in London in 1936 where he remained until his death the following year.

Snakes Alive

There was a shock discovery when brewing commenced in Nigeria in 1960. Snakes liked to crawl into the empty transportable tanks while they lay at Lagos awaiting return to Dublin. Most of the snakes expired in the cold Irish climate, but in summer there could be survivors. Apart from keeping the cleaners alert, the Dublin Zoo was kept well supplied with new exhibits. Unlike Lagos, Dublin did not have a resident snake catcher.

The Number-takers

Brewery notes contain numerous entries making arrangements for the return of casks. They were fairly valuable and could easily be

Number-takers recorded and tracked the number of each cask dispatched.

misdirected or even used by another brewer. Each of the half a million wooden barrels and casks in the brewery had a number cut into the head for traceability. When that full barrel left the site the number was recorded and similarly when it returned. Draymen spent hours taking the numbers before each barrel was delivered to the pub. Non-return of an empty could be traced on the books and the publican would be requested by letter to return the barrel. If he failed to do so a bill would be sent. This discouraged cutting up barrels to make feeding troughs or rainwater butts. Similarly if a cask was determined foul by the sniffers, having been used to store oil or petrol, the last user could be traced. A weekly bonus ('beefer money') was paid to the number-takers for accuracy and avoidance of mistakes.

Eventually two changes made number-taking a fruitless task. Change to metal kegs and higher labour costs made the employment of fifty number-takers and the delay to deliveries uneconomical. Beer became the publicans' property when it left the brewery, but the casks remained brewery property. In September 1922, the height of the civil war brought an important notice to customers:

> The frequent cessation of both road and rail transport since June last created a serious situation and unless every trader makes a special effort to return our casks directly they are empty we may shortly find ourselves without sufficient casks to supply their requirements. Under our trade terms each trader is responsible for the prompt return of empty casks at his own expense to the station or berth from which they are ordinarily dispatched to Dublin, to bear a portion of the extra cost of cartage to secure a quick return.

Beer was seized in April 1922 from a canal boat at Quaker Island, near Carrick-on-Shannon, and more at Kenmare. A quantity stolen from a train by armed men resulted in a letter: 'We are prepared to share the loss with Mrs O'Regan and propose therefore only charging her half of the invoiced price in connection with the loss of the cask.'

The Wages Train

Each Friday the men in the Lower Level cooperage, traffic and racking were paid in cash at the Lower Level cash office. This involved moving a safe on a special narrow gauge railway bogie from the main cash office in the front yard down the spiral railway descent and through the tunnel under James's Street. For security the brewery gates would be closed on a signal sounded by sirens on the roof of the front offices and on the power station. They sounded at five minutes before twelve to close all gates and at twelve o'clock to indicate that they could be reopened as the safe had reached its destination secure within the Lower Level cash office. The trains ceased operation in 1962, but the siren sounded its ghostly wail for the long departed cash train until the power station became decommissioned in the late 1990s. It must have been carefully maintained, because it allowed for summer time each year.

Wages were transported in a safe mounted on a railway wagon from the cash office to the wages office on the lower level.

Messengers

Messengers were a vital service within the site until the 1960s. On their first day in the brewery they would be sent to McBirney's to be measured for their uniforms. Decked out in livery with pill-box caps, they stood to attention outside the door of important people ready to carry a message anywhere throughout the brewery. Messengers

Liveried messengers carried post through the brewery.

also had to answer the bell and come up to an office if the fire needed coal. In the long moments awaiting a call the messengers entertained themselves with a series of pranks.

One of these was to undress an unfortunate messenger, place him in the lift and dispatch him to an upper floor to his mortal embarrassment and the loudly expressed horror of the lady clerks.

Cats were kept at the brewery to control the rodent population. Each day a messenger was sent to the staff restaurant to collect a bucket of fish heads for the cats. The poor lad would stroll across the yard like the Pied Piper followed by an army of hungry cats. A strict number of felines were on the books for each department and a board order intoned: 'the authorised establishment of brewery cats must be strictly adhered to.' This memo was passed down the chain of command from directors to brewers and thence to managers, one of whom posted it on the notice board with the endorsement: 'senior tomcat to note'.

Lads

Boys joined the business after the brewery examination, often held at the Masonic Hall when their results would be endorsed 'son of an outsider', because sons of employees were given preference. Boys were destined for promotion to 'Lads' and ultimately to pensionable employment as men subject to satisfactory performance. In poor times the wage of a boy was welcome in any household, but the Christian Brothers were dismayed to see their star pupils commence labouring work when they were capable of third-level education.

Lads who misbehaved would be sent to apply red-, blue- or green-coloured raddle (paint) on filled casks – a filthy job.

Excise

Duty and excise payments are a fundamental part of brewery life. Duties on beer and malt accounted for, and still make up, the majority of the price of beer in Britain and Ireland. Initially the duty was levied on malt and strict controls applied to the possession and movement of malt. A revenue act in 1782 required record keeping, permits for movement and sworn evidence on quantities of malt made.

An act was passed in 1819 to copperfasten the collection of the duties on malt and to amend the laws relating to brewers in Ireland. This act forbade the use of liquorice and colouring (burnt sugar) and any form of sugar on a brewery premises.

The surveyors who worked for the Commissioners of Customs and Excise were zealous in their pursuit of undutied beer and illicit substances to the point of breaking the law. In 1764, 1766 and again in 1767 a Robert Bray, an excise surveyor, broke into the St James's Gate brewery in search of undutied beer. He was arrested and received a fine of £20 and a sentence of one week's imprisonment for his efforts, but he also received two guineas bounty for each of the twenty-one illegal stills which he seized during the raids.

On 17 June 1767 a riot also occurred in Leixlip, in the same street as Arthur and Samuel Guinness's brewery, illustrating the venom in the battle between distillers, brewers and the excisemen. The riot broke out when George Gann a gauger (custom's official) fixed a fine notice for £50 to the person of John Whelan, a distiller. The extent of the riot may be deduced from the compensation claims on the Commissioners for Excise. Gann claimed £11 for the loss of a horse and the attendance of a farrier for seventeen days, presumably before the horse died of its injuries. A further claim for broken windows and furniture, as well as the expense of prosecuting John Whelan and the rioters cost £12. The Commissioners wrote to the authorities seeking to have a party of the army quartered in Leixlip to support the excisemen.

The 1819 Malt Duties' Act remained until 1880 when the excise act, known as the 'Relieved Mash Tuns Act', changed the materials that could be used in beer and introduced the concept of payment of duty based on the sugar 'declared' in the fermenting vessel.

From that time malt had to be reconciled with brews. Fermenters were declared and dipped (depth measured) as soon as they were full, but before the fob became so abundant that it came out the doorway. The accuracy was not perfect. A deviation of an inch either way represented hundreds of pounds in duty gained or lost.

A wastage allowance of 6% was permitted and it was a point of honour that actual waste should not reach anything approaching this figure. If a spillage occurred the excise would be called to witness the damage and if appropriate grant a rebate. Brewers were given rebate of excise when there was loss of excise-paid beer due to flooding, fires, bursting of vessels etc. On reporting a possible claim for rebate of duty the first question that would arise 'was the merchant negligent?'. This was a serious question because in the event of negligence no rebate would be granted. Since 1990 duty is paid at the time the beer leaves the site and much of the measurement and reconciliation is redundant.

Purser Family

Three generations of the Purser family – John, John Junior and John Tertius – were all directly involved in St James's Gate. John Purser came from Tewkesbury in Gloucestershire and moved to London where he established himself as a brewer in Leather Lane and at Hackney. His business did not prosper due to lack of working capital and in 1776 he was working at Reid's brewery at Fishpond Street, London.

On the invitation of Robert Barnewall, he moved to Dublin in that year to work with a Dublin-based brewer, James Farrell of Blackpitts. It is clear that John Purser brewed porter commercially in Dublin in 1776, but not certain that this was the first Dublin porter.

Faulkner's Dublin Journal of June 1740 claims that 'the porter brewed in Dublin greatly excels that which is imported from London'. While not mentioning the brewer, the next issue names the taverns where the porter could be enjoyed. Thwaites' brewery petitioned the Irish Parliament in 1763 to assist the production of porter in Ireland, which they said they had perfected. In the absence of the assistance they became importers of English porter. About 1778 Arthur Guinness commenced brewing porter. Six brewers and Mr Barnewall wrote testimonials dated July 1781,

BELOW: Heroic pose of a cooper amidst wood shavings in the cooperage at St James's Gate.

shortly after John Purser's death.

Barnewall wrote:

I engaged Mr John Purser in London to come to Dublin to brew porter for Mr Farrell and I was informed on a very strict inquiry that he was perfectly capable and was very able in that business.

The other testimonials came from Mr Farrell, PH Sweetman, George Thwaites, Thomas Andrews, Nathaniel Warren and Edward

85

Atkinson. The reason for these testimonials is not clear. They could have been obituaries or might have been for the purpose of transferring royalties to his son. Though there was no testimonial from Arthur Guinness, there were connections. A deed of 1780 has Purser's son as a party and Arthur Guinness granting the deed for property.

John Purser died in 1781 at Rathcormac en route to Cork to investigate the potential for his services there. He left three sons one of whom, John, joined the St James's Gate brewery about 1786 but fell out with Arthur Guinness. However, in 1799 he was taken back by the second Arthur as a book-keeper and his son, John Junior, also joined the brewery, in the same year, as an apprentice brewer. John Junior Purser signed the advertisement attesting to the quality of Guinness porter in 1814.

By an agreement dated 1 February 1820, John Purser and John Junior were partners in the St James's Gate brewery with the Guinness family. They were partners in the business but not in the ownership of the buildings.

John Tertius, the third generation, was born in 1809 and became head brewer at the James's Gate brewery in 1858. When Edward Cecil Guinness bought out his brother, Arthur Edward Guinness, in 1876 he depended heavily on John Tertius and tried to get him to become a partner. John Tertius retired when the brewery was floated as a public company and ceased to be privately owned in 1886. He had been allocated fewer shares than the newly appointed financier Herman Hoskier. On his retirement he reminded Edward

Cecil Guinness that as part of an agreement with his grandfather he was entitled to receive a shilling per barrel brewed since about 1780. This yielded £217,196 in the context that the whole company was valued at £6 million. He died at the Purser family home, Rathmines Castle in 1893.

The Purser family married into the Geoghegan family, another very influential family in the brewery's history. At one stage, two Geoghegan brothers, William and Samuel, were Head Brewer and Head Engineer respectively. Samuel was the inventor of the Geoghegan locomotive used on the narrow-gauge railway. William quarrelled with Edward Cecil Guinness over his percentage and got a rise to three shillings per hundred hogsheads.

Sarah Purser, daughter of John Tertius, was an accomplished artist and painted the cooperage at St James's Gate. Purser's son-in-law, John Purser Griffith, became a leading Dublin Port and civil engineer and developed the water and electricity works at Poulaphuca. When he died in 1938 the coopers from St James's Gate requested permission to carry his coffin the last stretch of the journey to Whitestown cemetery in Rathfarnham, County Dublin.

Local Bottling in Pubs

Publicans bottled their own beer in their premises from barrels and hogsheads delivered by the company before a central bottling plant was established at the brewery in the late 1970s. The method was fairly primitive but effective. The barrel would be manoeuvred onto a wooden platform – the stillon – and the vent bung on the cask

Beer casks are lowered into cool underground pub cellars to maintain optimum condition.

would be opened by hammering it inward. A special tool at the brewery was used to recover the bungs from inside the empties. Then a brass tap was struck through the outlet bung so that after the initial gush it sealed against the wood of the barrel. The flat beer was then poured into a trough attached to siphons and the bottles filled, corked and labelled by hand. The beer contained yeast and gyle (unfermented wort) so carbon dioxide gas evolved as the beer conditioned in the bottle over about ten days. Bottling had to be prompt, otherwise the beer would condition in barrel and form too much fob to bottle. This beer was not pasteurised and the growing yeast removed oxygen. Some aficionados believed that this bottle-conditioned product was superior to all others. The product was replicated in factory production, but a pasteurised product took over to deliver the longer shelf life demanded by retail outlets.

Hoggers

Empty barrels and hogsheads were stacked on the quays both at Custom House and at City Quay. Sheltered from view, there was the shady world of the 'hoggers'. This group of vagrants assembled on the dockside around the empties returning from the British market and consumed the dregs of the barrels that were available. The barrels were marked with red paint to indicate their contents and this paint, or raddle, was a particular red colour. These characters were also known as 'raddlers', as it was suggested that their faces and beards were stained red from the raddle on the casks. The police would disperse them when they became excessively rowdy. 'Spunkers' were a variety on the theme; they drank from overflowing barrels and casks that had frothed over in hot summer weather. Similar groups of 'woodeners' or 'boilers' targeted empty whiskey casks that they scalded with boiling water to extract the last of the spirit from the wood.

The mainline train was led
by a man with a red flag
from the brewery into Kingsbridge (Heuston) station goods'
yard, to distribute kegs around
the country.

The Train

Each morning a train of wagons full of Guinness beer exited from the gate on St John's Road and wound its way past Heuston Station buildings and into the goods shunting yard for distribution by trains around the country depots. The train was led by a man on foot carrying a red flag. The Locomotives Act of 1865 (also known as the Red Flag Act) was introduced by the British Parliament as one of a series of measures to control the use of mechanically propelled vehicles on British public highways. The Act required 'at least three persons shall be employed to drive or conduct such a locomotive ... one of such persons ... shall precede such locomotives on foot by not less than sixty yards and shall carry a red flag constantly displayed and shall warn drivers and riders of horses of such locomotives.'

In 1896 the Locomotives on the Highway Act did away with the need of three persons and the man walking in front of the vehicle. In celebration the London to Brighton car run commenced. The Guinness brewery carried on using a man walking in front of the train. Despite this observance of the defunct red flag regulation, there was an accident. Each morning a steam roller departed from the Corporation depot on the quays bound for routine work at the Ballyfermot dump. The Guinness train and the Corporation steamroller shared their route along St John's Road. One fateful morning, about 1965, irresistible force met immovable mass and the train moving at walking pace led by its flagman and the steamroller at full speed of seven miles (eleven kilometres) per hour collided. Luckily nobody was hurt. At the subsequent court case it was alleged that the steamroller driver, Tempo, gave evidence that the train had swerved.

Reward

A notice in the *Freeman's Journal* of 24 August 1837 proclaimed a reward for the discovery of the perpetrators of an atrocious outrage:

> Whereas Thomas Kilduff, carrier left town on Saturday the 18 instant with Porter which he purchased at our brewery and was stopped near Curre's stream, in the county of Dublin, by six men, who alighted out of a covered car, in which they had pursued him, and immediately dragged said Kilduff to the ground where one of them placed his foot on his neck and threatened to dash out his brains with a crowbar, while the others proceeded to stave in the four casks which contained said porter, and which they accomplished. Now we the undersigned being fully determined to bring to punishment the ruffians who committed this outrage, and also those parties who are from mercenary motives supposed to have instigated them to the act (which is the second of a similar nature) do hereby offer a reward of a hundred pounds to any person who shall, within three calendar months prosecute to conviction the persons who committed the said act or those who may have instigated them to its commission. Or the sum of fifty pounds for such private information that will lead to the discovery or conviction of any of the parties concerned.

A.R. Guinness Sons & Co.

The destruction of the beer suggested a sinister anti-competitive motive that is emphasised by the substantial reward offered.

Fatal Accident at Brewery – Inquest

For many working in the brewery was a physical and demanding vocation. For some it even proved to be highly dangerous.

The *Freeman's Journal* on 6 December 1839 recorded an inquest on a terrible accident:

An inquest was held yesterday by Alderman Perrin on the bodies of the two unfortunate men, John Brien and William Campbell, who lost their lives on the previous day by descending into a vat containing a quantity of foul air. It appeared that Brien, who was what is called a porter finer, went into the vat on Wednesday about four o'clock to prepare for some process connected with his business, and in doing so the candle which he held in his hand was quenched by the foul air. On his ascending to light it he met a man named Daly, who warned him of the danger of going down again, to which the unfortunate man paid no attention, and immediately descended. He had not been an instant in the vat when he fell, upon which Daly, who saw him, ran for assistance, and when he came back found a number of men trying to drag him up by means of cords hooks etc., but to no effect. Campbell the other victim, then went down to rescue his comrade, and died instantly. Mr Purser, one of the company, stated that it was against all regulation of the establishment for any man to go into these vats at all. The jury

🍺 *The brewery maintained a fire brigade, perhaps because of the previous fires and the family involvement in insurance.*

returned that death was caused in consequence of their going into a vat, of their own free will, and against the rules of the establishment.

The Fire

The *Freeman's Journal* of 17 February 1820 carried an advertisement thanking their neighbours for timely assistance when there was a fire at the brewery. The response from private and insurance company fire engines prevented serious damage. The list includes the main brewers and distillers in the area, as well as other neighbours. Such co-operation was essential because the densely packed buildings were a serious fire risk. Insurance companies and parishes maintained fire-fighting equipment while everyone available helped extinguish a fire for fear it would spread to their own premises.

> Messrs A.B. and W.L. Guinness and Co. are anxious to return their most sincere and grateful thanks to all who so kindly and zealously exerted themselves in assisting to extinguish the fire which accidentally occurred at their brewery this morning, and also to the agents of the several insurance companies who early attended with their engines and firemen and were eminently active and successful. Messrs Guinness and Co. have the happiness to assure their friends that ... the fire which at first appeared extremely alarming, was under the blessing of Providence very quickly extinguished, and that the damage done is not very extensive, nor of such a nature as to stop the business of the brewery even for a day ...

> They cannot conclude without acknowledging the kind feeling, and the extremely orderly and good conduct evinced by the populace upon the occasion, which was such as to render the assistance of the police or military quite unnecessary.

The Loss of the *Barkley*

The *WM Barkley*, the first Guinness company steam ship, was destined to make her final fated journey during the First World War. She set out from Dublin bound for Liverpool on 12 October 1917.

En route in the Irish Sea, the ship was torpedoed and sunk by a German submarine, the *U75*, captained by Commander Lohs. The captain and five men were lost, leaving three men with Thomas McGlue, who gave this account:

> The submarine slipped away and we were left alone adrift in a boat, with hogsheads of stout bobbing all around us. The *Barkley* had broken and gone down very quietly. We tried to row for the Kish (light vessel) but it might have been America for all the way we made. We got tired and my scalded hand was hurting. We put out the sea anchor and sat there shouting all night.
>
> At last we saw a shape coming up. She was the *Donnet Head*, a collier bound for Dublin. We got in to Dublin about 5 a.m. and an official put us in the Custom House at the point of the wall where there was a big fire. That was welcome because we were wet through and I had spent the night in my shirtsleeves. But we weren't very pleased to be kept there three hours. Then a man came in and asked 'are you aliens'. Yes, we're aliens from Dublin. He seemed to lose interest then, so we walked out and got back into the lifeboat and rowed it up to Custom House Quay. The superintendent produced a bottle of brandy and some dry clothes and sent the gunner off to hospital to have his leg seen to. The rest of us went over to the North Star (hotel) for breakfast. And, later, after I'd had my arm dressed – the doctor said the salt water had done it good – the superintendent gave me a drayman's coat to wear and put me in a cab. I was glad to get back to Baldoyle, because I'd left my wife sick and was afraid she'd hear about the torpedoing before I could get home.

The period of the Second World War (1939–45) also saw some perilous narrow escapes for the Guinness vessels. The following account was recorded on 31 July 1941:

> The *Guinness* engaged a low flying aeroplane with her Hotchkiss guns at about 2.30 a.m. on July 17th when in about the same position as was the *Carrowdore* when she was attacked on 15th, no bombs were dropped.

Danger on the Liffey

In another incident the brewery barge *Docena* sank near the Custom House in 1927. The skipper B Holcroft describes meeting a sudden squall as he passed under Butt Bridge. He discovered he was in danger due to the amount of water shipped. He made for the pier but the mooring ropes had only been fixed when the barge sank. The men aboard scrambled ashore without injury. Only 167 of the cargo of 200 hogsheads of Guinness beer were saved. Two days later the barge was raised by the Dublin Port and Docks Board and found to be undamaged.

The SHANNON was a double-bowed lighter
with the engine placed to the side.

TRANSPORT

The Canals

In the late eighteenth, early nineteenth centuries Guinness beer sales expanded at a time of transport evolution when canals enjoyed their short-lived heyday. The Grand Canal supplied water to Dublin from 1769. With the completion of the fuller network from 1796, the canal replaced roads as the transport route to the interior of Ireland. Roads were almost impassable in winter and difficult enough during the rest of the year.

The canals brought about a steep change, permitting 50-ton loads of malt and barley to come into the city centre pulled easily by a single horse. This led to a network of canal-side maltings and grain stores throughout the country. The return trip carried loads of beer to all but the remotest corners of the country.

Barrels of beer loaded on barges could reach the River Barrow navigation at Robertstown and travel to Waterford. The Shannon navigation was reached at Bannagher and thence to Limerick.

Canal transportation centralised beer production that had hitherto been at pub breweries. It also facilitated excise control of the small breweries that had been previously widely dispersed.

Barges

There were two types of barges used to carry Guinness beer. The canal barges carried barrels of beer to places on the canal system from Grand Canal Harbour, at the rear of the brewery. In addition malt and barley were transported from places like Athy to the brewery basin adjoining the Robert Street grain store. Prior to construction

Crane loading barges at Victoria Quay jetty.

of the Victoria Quay wharf on the River Liffey in 1870, barges would have travelled from the Grand Canal Harbour to the Grand Canal docks at Ringsend.

The Liffey barges 1873–1961, or more correctly lighters, were bigger craft. They plied the Liffey from Victoria Quay to the Custom House, where the brewery ships were berthed. They operated in a narrow tidal window of an hour during rising tide and an hour during falling tide. This gave them enough water to float while allowing passage under the bridges. In order to fit under the bridges the barges had no superstructure or mast. The funnel was hinged so that it could be lowered as the barge passed beneath the bridge. These Liffey barges were replaced by trucks in 1961.

The LADY GRANIA and the Guinness barges, CASTLEKNOCK and KILLINEY.

A tight fit — the barges, or lighters, bound for the Custom House Quay in Dublin port could only navigate when the tide in the River Liffey was high enough to float them but low enough to allow passage under the bridges.

Coming of the Railway

When the railway age came to every town in Ireland in the 1840s and '50s, the brewery was again quick to exploit the new transport. Sidings were established directly into the brewery, while internal transport was mechanised by construction of an extensive internal narrow gauge railway. Designed by Guinness engineer Samuel Geoghegan, the internal railway system was a feature of the St James's Gate and surrounding streets until 1961. These trains brought coal to the furnaces and grain from the maltings and stores to the brewhouse. Spent grain was shuttled from the brewery to farm carts for animal feed.

In the 1970s rail transport was made more efficient by the use of cages of kegs that could be lifted from train to local delivery trucks. The brewery supplied country depots by special trains until September 2006. Originally the mainline trains entered the brewery by a spur line laid along St John's Road from Heuston Station. Later trucks carried large cages of kegs to the trains at Heuston Station.

Planet locomotive draws grain wagons within the brewery.

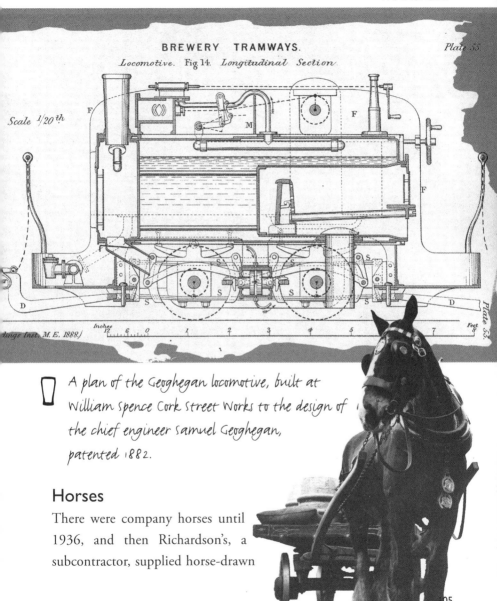

BREWERY TRAMWAYS.

Locomotive. Fig 14. *Longitudinal Section*

Plate 55.

Scale 1/20th

A plan of the Geoghegan locomotive, built at William Spence Cork Street Works to the design of the chief engineer Samuel Geoghegan, patented 1882.

Horses

There were company horses until 1936, and then Richardson's, a subcontractor, supplied horse-drawn

Horse-drawn delivery to Kehoe's on South Anne Street, c1960.

Horses bringing hop pockets to St James's Gate in the early days.

transport until 1960. Trace-horses were used to assist the heavily laden carts of beer up the steep hill at Stevens' Lane to deliver to pubs on the south side of the city.

Motor Transport

Early in the twentieth century the brewery adopted motor transport. Change was constant, wooden butts and hogsheads were replaced by transportable tanks, then 20-foot ISO containers and finally 30-ton loads in roll-on roll-off trailers. Today's 30-ton road tankers contain 300 hectolitres of beer – nearly 60,000 pints.

Malt transporter, c1960.

Straker Squire petrol lorry, 1909.

A·GUINNESS, SON & Co Ltᴰ

RI·1732

Leyland steam wagon, 1909.

INSET: Thornycroft steam wagon, 1899.

SON & Cº LIMITED DUBLIN.

Maritime Transport

Exports were part of the Guinness beer trade from the early days and grew in quantity and significance. Small quantities of Guinness beer were shipped to England (1796), Isle of Man (1810), Lisbon (1811), Liverpool (1812), Bristol (1819), Channel Isles (1822). West India porter was developed from 1801. These exports would all have been carried in sailing ships.

Steamship trade to West Africa began in 1852, with the formation of the British and African Navigation Company. The trade was in cocoa and cotton, and the southern Nigerian railway was

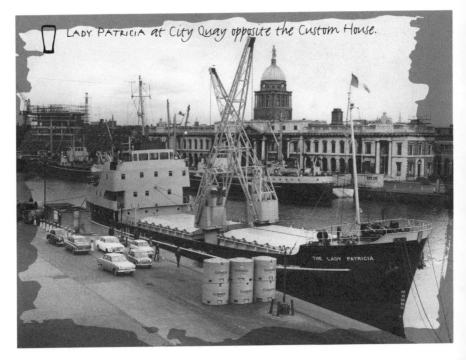

LADY PATRICIA at City Quay opposite the Custom House.

SS GUINNESS *raising steam prior to departure for Liverpool.*

constructed as a colonial development venture. The Elder Dempster line formed in 1879 from these earlier companies, and was closely associated with trading Guinness beer in West Africa and the Caribbean. The bottling company of MacAfee was acquired in 1932. They specialised in ship's stores and Foreign Extra Stout became a favourite among ships' crew. McAfee distributed to West Africa, while a consortium, Export Bottlers, supplied the trade to India and Egypt.

The regular shipping lines, such as Bristol Steam Navigation Company, Clyde Steamship Company, Burns & Laird Line and British & Irish Steam Packet Company also carried Guinness beer exports to the UK.

'Ship Shape and Bristol Fashion'

Dublin was beset by industrial unrest in 1913, culminating in the General Strike led by Jim Larkin the labour leader. Shipping and the docks were a prime focus of the unrest. The company had used all manner of shipping up to that time but in order to secure their trade, the firm decided to operate their own ships.

The *WM Barkley* was purchased from Kelly's of Belfast around the time when Dublin port was disrupted by the general strike of 1913. While en route from Dublin to Liverpool on 12 October 1917, the *Barkley* was torpedoed and sunk by the German submarine *U75*. Four of the crew were lost. The wreck lies in 45 metres just on the east side of the Kish Bank, Dublin Bay.

Three colliers, *Carrowdore*, *Clarecastle* and *Clareisland*, were bought from Kelly's of Belfast and replaced by the *SS Guinness* and later by the *Ladies Grania*, *Gwendolen* and *Patricia* and finally the *Miranda Guinness*. Named after the wife of the Earl of Iveagh, the *Miranda Guinness* was the last ship built at Hill's of Bristol whose crest bore the motto 'shipshape and Bristol fashion'.

Typically the ships transferred beer to road tankers at Wiggs' Wharf on the Manchester Ship Canal near Runcorn. Earlier ships would go up into Pomona Dock at Manchester or as far afield as Bristol and London.

After eighty years, changes brought about by containerisation and roll-on-roll-off trade offered more flexibility than company-owned ships.

Shipboard

Though there was a brewery aboard the converted Blue Funnel liner *Menestheus* briefly during the Second World War, the *Lady Patricia* may claim to be almost unique as a floating brewery. The *Lady Patricia* was the first ship adapted with beer tanks to carry beer in bulk. The conditioning of the beer was completed during the voyage. The ship's tanks were washed and steam sterilised en route back to Dublin, after the beer had been discharged at Runcorn or Liverpool.

On one occasion as the *Patricia* entered a lock on the Manchester Ship Canal, the captain looked over the side and, to his horror, the lock was filling with frothy tank washings. Someone had started to discharge the rinsings of beer before they had reached the open sea. The authorities were very strict about discharges in the canal which was suffering from serious pollution of all types and was filthy. He had to think quickly and ordered 'full ahead on engines, full astern, stop engines'. The engines obeyed and the propellers churned up the filthy mud from the bottom of the lock. The stinking ordure that was disturbed concealed the beer foam and nobody was the wiser.

The task was more advanced another day and the tanks were being steamed. Whatever following wind conditions prevailed the ship was shrouded in clouds of steam as it made its way past the South Stack and out to sea toward Dublin. An aeroplane passing overhead observed this strange sight and promptly reported that the *Patricia* was on fire, and a lifeboat was launched to assist before all was declared safe.

The *Miranda* had a collision with the East Link toll bridge on the Liffey while outward bound one day. It was thought that her bow thruster had caused her to deviate from her course.

More seriously on 10 November 1961 the *Lady Gwendolen* ran down the *Freshfield* lying at anchor during fog in the Mersey. The incident is widely quoted in Maritime case law. Ironically the *Lady Gwendolen* (then called *Paros*) was herself rammed and sunk at anchor on 10 November 1979 at Ravenna.

Loading a ship with wooden barrels.
INSET: Guinness train draws mainline railway wagons from Kingsbridge (Heuston) station into lower yard, about 1960.

The crew of the FANTÔME with Arthur Edward Guinness and his daughters seated in the front row.

MANSIONS
& YACHTS

 Guinness Estates

The Guinness family dwellings became legendary as befitted such a prosperous family. It was only a small exaggeration when said that you could walk from Chapelizod to Clonsilla – three miles (four and a half kilometres) – without stepping off Guinness family estates.

Beaumont

In the early days of the dynasty, shortly after his marriage in 1761 to Olivia Whitmore, Arthur Guinness made the move to Dublin and was elected Warden of the Corporation of Brewers in 1763. A year later he was living in style at Beaumont, County Dublin.

Arthur Guinness's 'gentleman's' residence of Beaumont house, north County Dublin.

Arthur Guinness is believed to have later moved to Mountjoy Square, where he lived until his death in 1803.

Mountjoy Square

Arthur Guinness later leased a house at Mountjoy Square. Both he and his wife lived there until they died in 1803 and 1814 respectively. Mountjoy Square was laid out 1792–1818 and was, for a short time, the most fashionable address in Dublin. The area declined in part due to the Act of Union in 1800 and the Great Famine from 1845. Later, Henry Lunell Guinness, Arthur's son, lived on the square, at number 19, at the corner of Belvedere Place.

The Irish embassy, 17 Grosvenor Place, London; the lease was sold to the Irish Government by Lord Moyne.

121

The Guinness family had three houses at Grosvenor Place, London, overlooking the gardens of Buckingham Palace.

Grosvenor Place

Arthur Guinness's great-grandson, Edward Cecil Guinness (the first Earl of Iveagh) commenced a spending spree after the flotation of the brewery in 1886. Amongst his first acquisitions was 4 and 5 Grosvenor Place, London. These fine houses overlooking the gardens of Buckingham Palace provided a perfect base for the entertaining season. They were later demolished after wartime bomb damage. Lord Iveagh's sons also liked Grosvenor Place. Walter Guinness acquired number 11. Ernest Guinness (Lord Moyne) had number 17 – so large that today it accommodates the Irish embassy. Its long lease was given to the state in 1948–49 when the new Republic was declared. Lord Moyne also owned a Dublin residence, Glenmaroon House, on a lofty site overlooking the Liffey valley at Chapelizod.

Farmleigh

Farmleigh House and its 78 acres (31 hectares) of grounds was the residence of the Earls of Iveagh for more than a hundred years. It was purchased by Edward Cecil Guinness and enlarged in the 1880s to include a fabulous ballroom. Such was the style of living for the Guinness family in the late nineteenth century that the magnificent Farmleigh was given over for nannies, governesses and children, and as a venue for the Dublin season from 1 February to 17 March, and Iveagh House was suitable as a town residence in Dublin.

The clock tower at Farmleigh, built in 1880, is visible from the brewery on the western skyline. Folklore suggested that Lord Iveagh

Ernest Guinness had his Dublin residence at Glenmaroon, overlooking the Liffey at Chapelizod.

Farmleigh Clock Tower, from which it was speculated that Lord Iveagh could observe the workers in the St James's Gate brewery yard.

could see the workers in yard from this vantage point. This would have been entirely unnecessary as the family played an active role into the 1980s. The Irish government purchased Farmleigh from the Iveagh trustees for £22 million in 1999, and it is used as accommodation for visiting heads of state and is otherwise open to the public. The architects were James Franklyn Fuller and William Young.

Elveden Hall

Elveden Hall, comprising 23,000 acres (15,000 hectares) in the Suffolk countryside, is the seat of the Iveagh branch of the family and principal residence from 1896. At Elveden the Marble Hall was designed by Sir Caspar Purden Clarke and William Young for the First Earl of Iveagh, as a tribute to the Estate's Indian former owner – a Maharajah. The marble carvings were cut into the white Carrera marble by up to 600 craftsmen. The intention was to provide a venue suitable to entertain royalty as befitted an earl. There was only one fireplace in the marble hall and during formal Royal events it was known to freeze the guests who had to remain still for the proceedings.

Iveagh House

Iveagh House is now the Department of Foreign Affairs, as Rupert Guinness donated it to the Irish State in 1939. Originally two houses, numbers 80 and 81 St Stephen's Green were bought by Benjamin Lee Guinness in 1862. He combined them to form the

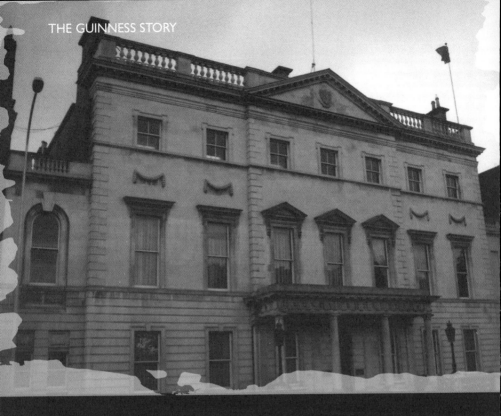

ABOVE: Iveagh House, St Stephen's Green,
Dublin, once the town house of Lord Iveagh,
now the Department of Foreign Affairs.
RIGHT: St Anne's in Clontarf, Dublin, was
the residence of Arthur Edward Guinness,
Lord Ardilaun.

current building, finished in Portland stone. The extensive Iveagh Gardens are now open to the public.

St Anne's

Sir Arthur Edward Guinness, great-grandson of Arthur Guinness, was born at St Anne's, Clontarf, on 1 November 1840. He was conservative MP for Dublin (1868–69 and 1874–80) then he became Lord Ardilaun. In 1880 he opened St Stephen's Green to the public. In 1870 the estate at St Anne's grew by acquisition to 496 acres (325 hectares). Queen Victoria visited St Anne's as part of her 1900 tour. During the Second World War St Anne's was used as an air-raid precautions store, and was later purchased by Dublin Corporation as a public park, reknown today for its rose gardens. The building was burned in an accidental fire and was demolished in the 1960s.

Ashford Castle, Cong, County Mayo, was Lord Ardilaun's country residence.

Ashford Castle

Sir Benjamin Lee Guinness, grandson of Arthur Guinness, acquired Ashford Castle, Cong, Co. Mayo, from the Oranmore and Browne family in 1852. He extended the estate to 26,000 acres (17,000 hectares), developing woodlands, gardens and roads. In 1868 Ashford was bequeathed to his son Arthur Edward Guinness, Lord

Ardilaun. In 1905 the Prince of Wales visited for a shoot. The Iveagh Trust owned the estate from 1915 to 1938 when it became a hotel.

On 13 October 1882, at the height of the 'Land War', Lord Ardilaun's bailiffs, Mr Hoddy and his grandson, were clubbed and shot, and their bodies dumped in Lough Mask while serving a process for an eviction at Mullagh. The murder happened in front of a crowd, several of whom were arrested.

Lord Ardilaun was also the only one to come to the assistance of Captain Boycott, Lord Erne's agent. Tenants struggling for a fair deal had refused to work the earl's harvest. Boycott had responded with evictions and other unpopular estate management measures. At the instigation of Charles Stewart Parnell, the whole county shunned Boycott and the affair was widely broadcast in all the newspapers of the time. Ardilaun continued to supply him with provisions transported on his lake steamer to the northern end of Lough Mask and then escorted by road to Boycott's house.

Luttrellstown Castle

In 1930 Arthur Ernest Guinness purchased Luttrellstown Castle in the Liffey valley, close to Dublin, as a wedding present for his daughter Aileen on her marriage to Brinsley Plunkett. Brinsley died as an airman in the Second World War. Aileen Plunkett left £96m when she died in 1999 – the largest will proved in the Irish probate courts at the time.

Yachting

In the 1880s yachting became popular among the smart set led by the Prince of Wales. Cowes week was the focus of lavish entertainment. The Guinness family took to the new fashion with gusto as befitted the new nobility. In the membership list of the Royal St George Yacht Club for 1924 the overall tonnage of yachts exceeding 5 tons was 3,893 and of this the Guinness family owned 1,538 tons. The Rear Commodore was the Hon AE Guinness, who personally owned 1,076 tons. One of his craft was a hydroplane, *Oma II*.

Fantôme II

The most magnificent was *Fantôme II*. The 611-ton barque, originally named *Belem*, was built at Chantenay-sur-Loire in 1896 by the Dubigeon shipbuilding company. She was ordered by the French industrialist Fernand Crouan to bring cocoa from Brazil for the Ménier chocolate factory. She continued this trade until 1914 when she was purchased by the Duke of Westminster, who refitted her as a luxury yacht. Arthur Ernest Guinness acquired her in 1921 and renamed her *Fantôme II*. In 1921 he took his daughters Aileen, Maureen and Oonagh on a round-the-world cruise. Decommissioned in 1939, the *Fantôme II* was abandoned in a creek at the Isle of Wight. An Italian foundation restored her as a sail training vessel in 1952, and she was bought by the *Belem* Foundation, sponsored by the French bank Caisse d'Epargne in 1980. Since then the *Fantôme II*, or *Belem*, has been based at Nantes

The FANTÔME, named back to its original name, BELEM, seen during the Tall Ships' Race at Waterford.

The stylish saloon aboard the FANTÔME.

as the last major French sailing ship. In 2005 she visited Waterford during the Tall Ships' Race and was photographed by John Colfer of Dunmore East.

The Ill-fated *Fantôme*

The keel of another vessel also called the *Fantôme* was laid in Livorno, Italy during the First World War. Designed initially as a destroyer, the hull lay unfinished. The Duke of Westminster ordered her completion as a 1,270-ton yacht, *Flying Cloud*, in 1927. She sailed the French Riviera in the Roaring Twenties. About 1938 Arthur Ernest Guinness acquired her. On his death in 1949, *Fantôme* was sold in Seattle but remained abandoned there for fourteen years. In 1956 the Greek shipping magnate, Aristotle Onassis, purchased her as a wedding gift for Prince Rainier and Princess Grace of Monaco, but when he was not invited to the wedding the ship lay abandoned at Kiel. She became a cruise ship in 1969 and operated for Windjammer Barefoot Cruises in the Caribbean. On 27 October 1998 the fated *Fantôme* sank off Guanja Island on the Honduran Coast during Hurricane Mitch. Captain March and all thirty West Indian crew were lost, but passengers had disembarked when their trip was cancelled due to the bad weather.

AMO and *AMO II*

Built in 1917 by Levis in Quebec as an anti-submarine boat, *ML 482, AMO II* was converted in 1928 by Arthur Ernest Guinness and brought to Cong. AE Guinness also acquired her sister ship, the *ML*

575, which he called *AMO*. The *AMO II* sailed Lough Corrib as a pleasure boat before falling into disuse. She became the last boat to sail through Galway's Eglinton Canal in 1954, before low bridges replaced the swing bridges and obstructed the waterway. Though refitted in Dún Laoghaire, the *AMO II* was not sold and was scrapped by Hammond Lane Company in 1954. The other *AMO* may have been used for spare parts and may lie submerged at Cong. The name *AMO* (Latin 'I love') is derived from the initials of his daughters, Aileen, Maureen and Oonagh.

Roussalka

The 1,400-ton Guinness yacht *Roussalka* sank on 1 September 1933 off Killary Harbour. The vessel under Captain Laidlaw had landed some guests at Killary bound for Ashford Castle. When the vessel was leaving the inlet he took a wrong course and struck Bloodslate Rock near Fraebl Island. All aboard, including Lord Moyne and crew of twenty-five, escaped without injury though she sank in eleven

LEFT: The ill-fated ROUSSALKA, sank after striking rocks off Killary Harbour, while sailing from Ashford Castle.

Lord Moyne was quick to replace the ROUSSALKA with another steamer converted into a luxury yacht, the ROSAURA, which went on to cruise the Mediterranean in the 1930s.

minutes. Originally named the *Brighton*, she was built by the Denny yard on the Clyde in 1903 as a railway steamer. Bought by Lord Moyne in 1930 she was refitted. A 500-ton oil tank was installed to enable her to cross the Pacific. Her turbines were replaced by diesels and one of her funnels was removed.

Rosaura

Within a month of the sinking of the *Roussalka*, Lord Moyne obtained the *Rosaura*, another Newhaven-to-Dieppe channel steamer that was lying disused at Newhaven. Built by Fairfield at Govan in 1905, the 1,210 ton, vessel was named *Dieppe IV*. During the First World War she served as a troopship and hospital ship. In September 1933 she was sold to Lord Moyne and converted to an ocean-going yacht. The 1933 refit included replacement of the Parsons steam turbines with Atlas Diesels, a funnel and third screw were removed, and the extra accommodation increased her registered capacity to 1,538 tons. Her appearance became uncannily like the *Roussalka*. In August 1934 Lord Moyne entertained the Prince of Wales and Mrs Simpson on a two-week Mediterranean cruise from Spain to Genoa to escape the attentions of the press. The next year Prince Edward became King Edward VIII and abdicated. The *Rosaura* was hired by the Admiralty as an armed boarding vessel in November 1939 and was mined and sank off Tobruk on 18 March 1941.

Private Aircraft

It was quite common for companies to have their own aircraft and the brewery was no different. It is described in a board document of 1975:

> The carrying capacity of the jet stream *200 G-BCGU* is 9 passengers plus two pilots; the aircraft is based at Leavesden (Watford). There are facilities for producing tea and coffee on board, Guinness beer and Harp will normally be carried.

PHILANTHROPY

St Patrick's Cathedral was rescued from a ruinous state by the donations of Benjamin Lee Guinness.

St Patrick's Cathedral and the Iveagh Trust

The Guinness family became fabulously wealthy on the flotation of the company in 1886. The new-found wealth was invested wisely in estates in Vancouver and stately dwellings, such as the Iveagh seat at Elveden in Suffolk, England. This wealth brought responsibilities with it, according to the family principles and the Victorian way of thinking. The family made significant contributions to many institutions in Dublin, and achieved recognition in return in the

form of the peerages Moyne, Iveagh and Ardilaun.

Early projects were the restoration of St Patrick's Cathedral and the adjoining Marsh's Library. In 1860 Benjamin Lee Guinness, grandson of Arthur Guinness, funded the start of work on the cathedral. The south wall was rebuilt, the south porch added and windows replaced. For the first time in centuries the internal space of the cathedral was opened up by the removal of screens and chambers. Lord Ardilaun and Lord Iveagh, sons of Benjamin Lee, carried on the work, restoring the choir and the bell tower and presenting the cathedral with a new organ and the park.

The Iveagh Trust especially was involved in housing and other facilities for workers. The slums of Dublin were infamous and the area around St Patrick's Cathedral was particularly bad. The solution was to build a large complex of apartments along with facilities including a swimming pool, a school, a hostel for the homeless and a crèche for children of working mothers. By 1895, 135 people were housed in Iveagh

SIR BENJAMIN LEE GUINNESS
BARONET LL.D
MEMBER OF PARLIAMENT
FOR THE CITY OF DUBLIN

RIGHT: Benjamin Lee Guinness statue at St Patrick's Cathedral. The Guinnesses are the only family to have two members commemorated by statues in Dublin.
LEFT: The Iveagh Trust buildings.

In 1901, the Iveagh Trust had entire blocks of dreadful slums demolished and replaced with a park, crèche, homeless hostel, school, swimming pool and apartments. The Iveagh Markets (TOP) were

buildings in Hammersmith, London and another 343 in Dublin. Housing schemes were built in London at Brandon Street, Draycott Avenue and Columbia Road. The Guinness Trust has continued its work more recently at Rochdale, Liverpool and Naish Court, London. The Dublin buildings were taken over by Dublin City Council in more recent years.

In 1880, the Rialto buildings were built to house workers by Dublin Artisan Dwellings company, which had associations with Guinness.

Lord Ardilaun

Lord Ardilaun (Arthur Edward Guinness) arranged to have St Stephen's Green made a public park – there had been plans to fill the square with buildings. In recognition a bronze statue of Lord Ardilaun by Thomas Farrell was erected on St Stephen's Green. He also served as MP for Dublin (1868–69 and 1874–80), completed restoration of Marsh's Library and rebuilt the Coombe hospital. He married Lady Olivia White, daughter of the Earl of Bantry, who is believed to have encouraged him to sell his interest in the brewery to his brother so that he would not be 'in trade'. This may have also facilitated his ennoblement. He purchased Muckross Estate, Killarney, which had been owned by her relations so that it would not be spoiled.

Kenwood House Collection

Edward Cecil Guinness, Lord Iveagh, assembled a significant collection of old masters' paintings while he was furnishing his London home at 4 and 5 Grosvenor Place, Hyde Park Corner. In the fifteen years after the flotation of the business in 1886, he parted with a half a million pounds, amassing the collection that only partly forms the Kenwood House exhibition.

Lord Ardilaun saved St Stephen's Green from property development.

The Iveagh Bequest saved Kenwood House on Hampstead Heath, London from demolition in 1925, and filled it with the Iveagh paintings as a public gallery. The bequest was the most important collection of private paintings ever donated to Britain. Lord Iveagh's collection includes a Rembrandt self-portrait, a substantial number of English paintings and Vermeer's *The Guitar Player*.

Kenwood House on Hampstead Heath showcases Lord Iveagh's art collection – the Iveagh Bequest.

The Moyne Institute

The Moyne Institute of preventative medicine at Trinity College is housed in a building presented to Trinity College, Dublin by Grania Guinness, in memory of her father, the first Baron Moyne. The building was designed by the architect Desmond Fitzgerald. In 1994 Grania Guinness, the Dowager Marchioness of Normanby, funded a major extension to the building.

Calypso

The well known marine exploration vessel *Calypso*, operated by Jacques Cousteau, had been bought by Guinness and leased to Cousteau for one franc per year. Loel Guinness sold it to Francine Cousteau for a Euro, but it was damaged at Singapore in 1996 and brought back to La Rochelle for preservation.

Care of the Workers

A medical department was established in 1888, from that time workers and their families had access to the company medical staff. Dr Charles Lumsden became the chief medical officer in 1899 and conducted social surveys of the workers' housing, sanitation and health. He cooperated with Sir Charles Cameron, the Public Analyst for Dublin. As a result the Iveagh Trust had the worst of the slums around St Patrick's Cathedral cleared and reconstructed. Houses were built at several locations around the city to accommodate workers. Family outings were arranged on Queen's Day to commemorate the visit of Queen Victoria in 1901, and each year thereafter until 1915. Subsequently, sports days were held at the Iveagh grounds and the last family day was held at Dublin Zoo in 1997. The bicentenary centre swimming pool at St James's Gate was presented to the workers as a gift from the family in 1959.

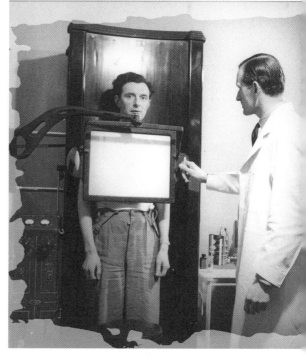

A medical centre provided care for workers and their families.

WARTIME

Brewery fire and rescue squads
training in gas masks during
the Second World War.

The Boer War

War and civil disturbance meant trying times for the brewery as well as every other business.

In 1900 Edward Cecil Guinness, first Earl of Iveagh, undertook to pay the cost of staffing a mobile hospital in South Africa for the Boer War. It was attached to Kitchener's 11th Division. At the outbreak of the war there were no mobile or static hospitals attached to the army, but eventually there were ten private hospitals. The ancillary staff, steward of stores compounders, clerks, watermen, cooks and ward masters comprised mainly employees of the St James's Gate brewery. Having spared no expense, it included the very best equipment including a Roentgen X-ray machine powered by a bicycle generator. There were also anti-toxins for diphtheria, typhoid, blood poisoning and snake bite. Stimulants, such as Champagne and brandy, were provided for the sick and wounded. The field hospital left Dublin on 22 January 1900, led by Sir William Thompson, surgeon-in-chief, formerly of the Richmond Hospital. Captain Rupert Guinness, son of Edward Cecil, accompanied the hospital himself. On their return service medals were given, by the Lord Lieutenant, to those who participated at a banquet in the Gresham Hotel. Rupert Guinness, who had served in the Boer War with the Irish Hospital Corps, unveiled a memorial at Glasnevin cemetery to two men who died from disease while on service with the hospital: Patrick Lawlor and Peter J Murphy.

First World War

The First World War seriously affected trade. There was no conscription in Ireland and so relatively few men joined the British Army. Nonetheless, many brewery workers were killed or wounded. Grain was scarce and the duty on beer was increased massively. The alcoholic strength of beer was reduced – some say to prevent accidents and increase productivity in the shell factories after lunchtime drinking. The brewery ship *WM Barkley* was torpedoed and sunk in 1917 with the loss of several lives.

The 1916 Rising

The Guinness company supported the British authorities in suppressing the 1916 insurrection. Brewery life was greatly discommoded by the capture of the General Post Office and other prominent buildings by the Irish Volunteers in 1916. Surprisingly, for such a commanding group of buildings, the volunteers made no effort to capture the brewery.

A picket of Dublin Fusiliers, under Captain McNamara, was placed in the Robert Street grain store as part of the force surrounding the South Dublin Union. The grain store was accessible by an iron bridge across the canal. Mr McMullen of the brewery informed Captain McNamara and his sergeant, Quartermaster Robert Flood, that the nightwatchman on duty would have access to the store via the bridge. However, confusion occurred on the night of 29 April 1916 when Captain McNamara became ill and was replaced by Lieutenant Lucas of King Edward's Horse. The night clerk, a Mr Rice, went to Robert Street with Lieutenant Warswick. Robert Flood, the nervous sergeant in charge of the picket, unable to recognise the officer and the watchman, held them prisoner and then had them shot. When Mr Rice failed to return to his lodgings at 101 James's Street, his colleague and housemate, Mr Dockery, became concerned. Mr Dockery then went with Lieutenant Lucas to the Robert Street grain store and again Sergeant Flood had both men shot dead. The sergeant was eventually disarmed by a Captain Mariott and Mr Williams. He was later court-martialled for murder but found not guilty. Lieutenants Lucas and Warswick were buried in Dublin Castle and exhumed in the 1960s. Lieutenant Lucas was reburied at the Blackhorse Avenue military cemetery.

Armoured Cars

At the instigation of management, thirty-two drivers loyally volunteered for military service and were issued army uniforms, although they remained civilians. The company sent twelve petrol lorries, three steam cars and two motorcars for army service. Two trucks were used at Portobello Hospital in Red Cross service. Three trucks were converted into armoured personnel

Grave of Lieutenant Lucas at Blackhorse Avenue military cemetery.

⬭ Armoured car, built by placing a railway engine smoke-box on a Guinness Daimler truck chassis. They were used to storm occupied buildings, in Dublin, during the 1916 Rising, by reversing up to the door so that troops could exit safely. Some of the loopholes are painted dummies to distract attackers' fire.

carriers for the use of the British Army. These were the invention of a 'Colonel Porter' and involved taking a brewery Daimler flat truck and placing a railway engine smoke-box on the back, to carry troops as well as armouring the cab. The engine parts were installed at the railway works in Inchicore. The purpose was to reverse up to occupied premises and protect troops storming buildings. These were believed to be the first such armoured personnel carriers ever used and went into action at Grattan Bridge on Thursday 27 April 1916.

Casualties

One brewery man, Mr Traynor, was killed fighting with the Volunteers. Another, Mr Carmien, was shot by British troops near the City Markets. Diligent inquiries were made as to whether he had been involved, but it was agreed that he was only returning from work. A Mr Stodart was killed working with St John's Ambulance, and the board decreed that this was in a private capacity and no concern of theirs. The brewery sent half of the fire brigade to fight a fire at Jervis Street Hospital, at the end of the Rising, and these men would also have been St John's Ambulance-trained men. Two men, Harbourne and O'Leary, were killed near Mount Street Bridge fighting with the Glasnevin and District Volunteer Corps. They had likely been acting as guides to the Sherwood Foresters, who had been landed at Kingstown (Dún Laoghaire) and their advance halted by rebel fire from Clanwilliam House, on the city side of Mount Street Bridge. Their loss may have been pivotal in the heavy casualties suffered by British forces at Mount Street Bridge. Their loyalty to the crown was rewarded with a gratuity to their widows of £25.

The Aftermath

Of the brewery workforce, forty-three men were imprisoned or deported to Frongoch or other prison camps in England. In all, eighty-five brewery employees were marked absent during the Rising. All those involved with the Irish Volunteers were dismissed. The Licensed Grocers and Vintners' Protection Society sought and were refused an audience with Lord Iveagh to make a case in favour of the dismissed men. Several unions and William Martin Murphy, proprietor of the *Independent* newspaper, also made representations to no avail.

The troubles continued to affect daily business at the brewery. When the Custom House was burned by the IRA in 1921, the blaze was so intense that the Liffey barges and the brewery's ship, the *Carrowdore*, were warped across the river to safety. Shortly afterwards, bargemen described the bullets and shells whistling over them when the Four Courts were under attack during the Civil War in the summer 1922.

Second World War

During the Second World War the *Carrowdore* was bombed en route to Liverpool. The bomb skidded across the ship's deck and exploded in the water, leaving the tailfin as a macabre souvenir. The *SS Guinness* was retained and used to transport barley to supply the Park Royal brewery.

Dublin was only bombed accidentally by the Germans on a few occasions during the Second World War. There was a high state of alert, as indicated by the air-raid watcher's hut complete with siren on the roof of the front offices. Beer was rationed during the Second World War in Ireland and regulars in pubs would eagerly anticipate deliveries. They were willing to drink the stout flat without gas even before the pub bottlers had the chance to cork the bottles, much less await the week-long conditioning in bottle.

ADVERTISING

A diverse selection of labels from some of the fifty countries where Guinness is brewed.

The Guinness Brand

Guinness brand advertising has always been cleverly structured and has, as a result, won many awards. Sponsorship has been focused on high profile events to maximise impact. Advertising of alcoholic products is strictly regulated nowadays, and any association with health-giving properties is forbidden.

The Guinness brand was amongst the first to register and defend trademarks. As early as 1845, in Arthur Guinness *v* Weston, Henry Weston, victualler and wine and spirits' merchant of London was charged with trademark infringement. The same year in Arthur Guinness *v* Jones, John Jones, publican, of London was charged with trademark infringement. In 1847 Guinness *v* Hornblower saw plaintiffs, Arthur Guinness, Benjamin Lee Guinness and John Purser, brewers of stout, of Dublin, Ireland sue William Hornblower, printer and engraver of London for trademark infringement by printing imitation labels. When pubs took in barrels of unconditioned beer and bottled it on their premises they applied a label provided from the company printing works with

Examples of publican bottlers' labels.

158

their name as bottler. Authenticity was assured by the clause in the bottling contract 'who bottle no other stout or porter'. On conviction for any infringement, it was the custom to have the defendant advertise his offence in the local and national press, as part of the settlement.

The Guinness beer bottle label changed with changing fashion. Branding by the bottler or variety was at one time as prominent as the beer branding itself.

A 'Head' in Advertising

The mystery behind the famous surge as the head forms on a pint of Guinness was partly elucidated by application of science. In 1999 Australian researchers claimed to have solved the puzzle why the gas bubbles appeared to descend while the pint of Guinness beer was surging. A computer model produced a complicated explanation. Later at Stanford a 750-frame-a-second camera showed that the rising column of liquid at the centre of the glass was sufficient to cause a counter current of falling liquid at the edges. Small bubbles caught in this down current descend only to rise again and form the creamy head on the beer. The duration and mechanism of the surge has been exploited in many of the advertisements with the sequence ending showing the head of a pint forming.

'Tá siad ag teacht'

One of the advertisements caught popular imagination – this was *'Tá siad ag teacht'* ('They are coming'). The advertisement was made by

Arks agency to promote Guinness beer in 1977. This television commercial was the forerunner of the anticipation idea. Set on the Aran Islands, the customers wait in a bar with a ticking clock the only sound. On arrival of a keg of Guinness beer aboard a currach, the bar comes alive. The final scene sees the rowers' currach set off for another keg with the single word in Irish, '*Arís*' ('again'), also having the meaning 'the same again' or as in the German '*noch einmal*'.

Dancing and Other Ads

Joe McKinny dancing in anticipation became quite a cult and the television advertisements were reinforced with a poster campaign. The accompanying music, *Guaglione* by the Prez Prado Orchestra, became a topical mobile phone ring tone. The screen saver was also very popular with people visiting the Guinness website.

In 1928 Benson's advertising agency won the Guinness advertising account and their illustrator, John Gilroy (1895–1985), went on to produce many iconic images for over thirty-five years. His first Guinness poster was printed in 1930. He is perhaps best remembered for his posters depicting a girder carrier and a wood cutter and for the Guinness animals which included a toucan, gnu, lion and kangaroo. The animals with their long-suffering zookeeper appeared on posters, press advertisements and merchandise from the 1930s into the 1960s. Many

have been revived since. Talent abounded in Benson's advertising agency. Dorothy L Sayers was only one of the script and rhyme writers working there.

Gilroy's animals were a feature of Guinness advertising.

FULL CIRCLE

After consideration of a Leixlip site a new Guinness brewhouse (*see left*) was constructed adjoining the Liffey on the lower level of the St James's Gate site. The fermentation plant was enlarged to accommodate production of the full range of Diageo stouts, ales and lagers such as Smithwicks, Kilkenny, Harp, Red Stripe and included contract brewing of Budweiser, Tuborg, and Carlsberg.

RIGHT: *The last barge transport to Limerick left the Brewery Harbour in 1960. The beer near the Canal Harbour, in Limerick, was considered particularly superior because of the conditioning in cask during the gentle transport.*

Acknowledgements

I thank all the people who assisted the production of this book with advice and suggestions, as well as providing photos and other images. I am also particularly grateful for help given in reading and checking the text for factual and typographical errors.

Guinness Brand Archive: Eibhlin Roche and Claire Hackett – archivists; Peter Walsh, historian, Dublin; Tom Halpin; Patrick Guinness; Barney Yourell; Tony Brennan; Dublin Corporation Pearse Street Library: Paddy Donovan; Douglas Appleyard, Percy Dunbavand, Brian J Goggin, Cormac Lowth, Kilian Harford, Peter Mason, Brendan O'Donnell, Martin O'Hanlon, Tony Rath, Bert Starkey, Geraldine Sweeney, Ron Younge, Dr Purser.

Picture Credits

The author and publisher have endeavoured to establish the origins of all the images used. If any involuntary infringement of copyright has occurred, sincere apologies are offered and the owners are requested to contact the publisher.

The majority of the photographs come from the Guinness Brand Archive. Others: Ian Broad (pp55,138), Edward J Bourke (p162), Michelle Burns (p23), Brian Cleare & John Colfer (p131), Ruth Delany (p163), Sam Ebikade (p31), Mike Graham (p28), Colin Parry (p30), Peter Pearson (pp60, 124, 143 (inset)), Southhampton City Council (pp118, 132), Robert Vance (p142-3 (top)), Dennis Drum, auctioneers, Malahide, for Kernoff drawing, photographed by Sheldon photos (p54).

Bibliography & Sources

Appleyard, Douglas S, *Green Fields Gone For Ever: The Story of Coolock and Artane Area*, published by Coolock Select Vestry, 1985.

Archer, Stella & Pearson, Peter, *The Royal St George Yacht Club,* 1987.

Alfred Barhard, *Noted Breweries of Britain and Ireland*, Vol. 3, Joseph Colston, 1890.

Bryan, J & Murphy, Charles JV, *The Windsor Story*, Granada, 1979.

Byrne, Al, *Guinness Times,* Town House, 1999.

Byrne, Michael, *The Market Street Storehouse*, 2001.

Cuneo, Terence, *Mouse and His Master, Life and Works of Terence Cuneo*, New Cavendish Books, 1977.

Davies, Peter N, *The Trade Makers: Elder Dempster in West Africa 1852–1972,* Allen & Unwin, 1973.

De Courcy, JW, *The Liffey in Dublin*, Gill & Macmillan, 1996.

Denisson SR, & Oliver McDonagh, *Guinness 1886–1939 from Incorporation to the Second World War*, Cork University Press, 1998.

Faulkner's Dublin Journal, June 1740.

Freeman's Journal, contemporary accounts.

Guinness, Michele, *The Guinness Spirit*, Hodder & Stoughton, 1999.

Guinness, Michele, *The Guinness Legend*, Hodder & stoughton, 1989.

Guinness, Jonathan, *Requiem for a Family Business*, Macmillan, 1997.

Guinness, Patrick, *Arthur's Round: The Life and Times of Arthur Guinness*, Peter Owens Publishing, 2007.

Halpin, Thomas B, 'History of Irish Brewing', *The Brewer* 1988.

Kinsella, Anthony, 'Lord Iveagh's Irish Hospital in South Africa', 1900, *Dublin Historical Record*, spring 2006.

Lee, J, 'Money and Beer in Ireland 1790–1875', *The Economic History Review*, New Series, Vol. 19, 1, 183–194, 1966.

Lynch, P and Vaizey, J, *Guinness's Brewery in the Irish Economy 1759–1876*, Cambridge University Press, 1960.

Matthias, Peter, *The Brewing Industry in England*, Cambridge University Press, 1959.

McGennis, Tim, 'The Guinness Barges', *Iris na Mara*, Vol. 1, no 2.

Mulally, Frederic, *The Silver Salver*, Granada, 1981.

Purser, Michael, *Jellett, O'Brien, Purser and Stokes – Seven Generations, Four Families*, Prejmer Verlag, 2004.

Sheaff, Nicholas, *Iveagh House*, Department of Foreign Affairs, 1979.

Walsh, Peter, *Guinness*, The Irish Heritage Series, Easons, 1980.

Stewart, John Watson, *Gentlemen's and Citizens' Almanac*, Dublin, 1761.

Walls, Timothy, 'An improvised armoured personnel carrier', *History Ireland*, March 2005.

Wilson, Derek, *Dark and Light*, Weidenfeld & Nicholson, 1998.

Appendix
Ownership of the St James's Gate Brewery

The corporate ownership of the St James's Gate brewery evolved as follows:

Giles Mee 1670–1693

Alderman Mark Rainsford 1693–1709

Mark Rainsford Junior 1709–1715

Paul Espinasse 1715–1750

Arthur Guinness 1759–1803

Arthur, (1803–1855), Benjamin (d1826) & William (d1842) Guinness.

Benjamin Lee Guinness 1858–1868

Arthur & Edward Cecil Guinness 1868–1876

Arthur (Lord Ardilaun) sold his share to Edward (Lord Iveagh) 1876

Guinness became a publicly a quoted company in 1886 on the London Stock Exchange.

Guinness acquired Bells whisky distillery in 1985 and Distillers Company Limited in 1986 associating Gordons gin, Johnnie Walker and nearly half of the Scotch whisky brands with the Guinness brand. Diageo became the name of the quoted company in 1997 following the merger of GrandMet and the Guinness brand. This joined the Baileys, Tanqueray, Pimms and Smirnoff brands to the company, Seagram's brands, Crown Royal, Captain Morgan and Sterling vineyards were acquired in a joint deal with Pernod Ricard in 2001. This deal saw Bushmill's distillery in Antrim transferred to Diageo in 2005. An association with Ketel 1 vodka was sealed in 2008.

Guinness Family Tree

This greatly simplified Guinness family tree traces the main (Lee) family, but it is impossible to ignore the Bankers (Rundell) branch, the Lunell branch and the missionary family descended from John Grattan. The complexity is due to large families, multiple marriages, and intermarriage between cousins and stepchildren. Extensive genealogies covering all branches are given in the book, *The Silver Salver*, Frederic Mulally, Granada, 1981.

Richard Guinness, 1690–1766 (Steward to Dr Price)

m1. Elizabeth Read, 1698–1742 (Daughter of William Read), m2. Elizabeth Clare, 1752

c1. Richard Guinness (brewer at Leixlip)

c2. Francis Guinness

c3. Elizabeth Guinness

c4. Arthur Guinness, 1725–1803 (Founder of the brewery at St James's Gate)

c5. Samuel Guinness, 1727–1795 (Arthur's partner in Hibernian Insurance)

c6. Benjamin Guinness

NEXT GENERATION

Arthur Guinness, 1725–1803 (Founder of the brewery at St James's Gate)

m. Olivia Whitmore 1742–1814

c1. Elizabeth Guinness, 1763–1847 (m. Lord Mayor of Dublin, Frederick Darley)

c2. Rev Hosea Guinness, 1765–1841 (Rector of St Werburgh's, Dublin)

c3. Arthur Guinness II, 1768–1855 (Took over management of the family brewery and became director of Bank of Ireland)

c4. Edward Guinness, 1772–1833 (Dublin Solicitor bankrupt by ironworks in Palmerstown and Lucan, his daughter married Arthur's third son)

c5. Olivia Guinness

c6. Benjamin Guinness, 1777–1836 (Joined brewery)

c7. William Lunell Guinness 1777–1842 (Director of Norwich Union Insurance)

c8. Louisa Guinness

c9. John Grattan Guinness

c10. Mary Anne Guinness

Samuel Guinness, 1727–1795

m. Sarah Jago, 1732–1794 (6 Aug 1753)

c1. Richard Guinness, 1755–1829

c2. Mary Guinness, b1759

c3. Samuel Guinness, 1761–1826

NEXT GENERATION

Elizabeth Guinness, 1763–1847

m. Frederick Darley, JP (Lord Mayor of Dublin) of Swanbrook

c. Susan Rebecca Darley

Rev Hosea Guinness, 1765–1841 (Rector of St Werburgh's Dublin for 30 years)

m. Jane Hart, 1777–1835 (1794) (2nd Daughter of Lt. Col. Simon Hart H.E.I.C.S.)

c1. Olivia Guinness

c2. Rev Arthur Guinness

c3. Margaret Guinness

c4. Edward Hart Guinness

c5. Jane Guinness

c6. Elizabeth Guinness

c7. Benjamin Guinness

c8. Simon Guinness

c9. Anne Guinness

c10. Harriet Guinness

c11. Mary Anne Guinness

c12. Francis Hart Vicesimus Guinness 1819–1891 (Magistrate and warden at Collingwood and Ashburton NZ. Went to India and then to New Zealand)

Arthur Guinness II, 1768–1855 (Took over management of the family brewery)

m1. Anne Lee, 1774–1817 (1793); m2. Maria Barker, 1783– (1821)

c1. Rev William Smythe Lee Guinness

c2. Arthur Lee Guinness

c3. Sir Benjamin Lee Guinness, 1798–1868 (Head brewer and heir to family brewery) Lord Iveagh

c4. Susanna Guinness, 1804–1836

c5. Mary Jane Guinness

c6. Louisa Guinness

c7. Anne Guinness

c8. Elizabeth Guinness

c9. Rebecca Guinness, 1814–1870 (m. 1844 Sir Edmund Waller of Co. Tipperary)

Edward Guinness, 1772–1833 (Dublin Solicitor)

m. Margaret Blair (1796)

c1. Arthur Blair Guinness

c2. Jane Guinness

c3. Richard Guinness

c4. James Guinness

c5. Edward Bolton Guinness

c6. Elizabeth Guinness, 1813–1865 (m. cousin Sir Benjamin Lee Guinness)

c7. Anne Rebecca Guinness

c8. Olivia Guinness

Olivia Guinness, 1775, unmarried

Benjamin Guinness, 1777–1836 (of Brookville)

m. Rebecca Lee (1804), –1819

c. Susan Jane Guinness, 1805–1861

William Lunell Guinness 1779–1842 (of Mountjoy Square, became director of Norwich Union insurance and partner in brewery)

m. Susanna Newton –1842

c1. Rev William Newton Guinness, 1811–1894

c2. Anne Rebecca Guinness, 1819–1881

Louisa Guinness, 1781–1809

m. Rev William Deane Hoare (1804–1823)

c. Olivia Hoare

John Grattan Guinness 1783–1850

m1. Susanna Hutton; m2. Jane D'Esterre (née Cramer, widow of Norcot
d'Esterre, killed by Daniel O'Connell in a duel on 31-1-1818)

c1. Rev Henry Grattan Guinness, b1835

c2. unknown

Mary Anne Guinness, 1787–

m. Rev John Burke (1809) (MP of Ballydugan, Galway, descendents became
agents for Guinness in USA and Australia)

NEXT GENERATION

Sir Benjamin Lee Guinness, 1798–1868 (Head brewer and heir to family
brewery, 1st Bart of St James's Gate)

m. Elizabeth Guinness, 1813–1865 (2nd daughter of Edward Guinness)

c1. Anne Lee Guinness, 1839–1889 (m. 4th Baron Plunkett, Archbishop of Dublin)

c2. Sir Arthur Edward Guinness, 1840–1915 (1st and last Baron Ardilaun)

c3. Benjamin Lee Guinness, 1842–1900 (Capt of the Royal Horse Guards)

c4. Sir Edward Cecil Guinness, 1847–1927 (1st Baron and Earl of Iveagh,
became the richest man in Ireland after floating the brewing company)

NEXT GENERATION

Anne Lee Guinness, 1839–1889

(m. 4th Baron Plunket, Archbishop of Dublin, 1863)

Sir Arthur Edward Guinness, 1840–1915 (1st and last Baron Ardilaun, MP for
Dublin 1868–69 and 1874–1880)

m. Olivia Hedges White (daughter of Early of Bantry)

Benjamin Lee Guinness, 1842–1900 (Capt of the Royal Horse Guards)

m. Lady Henrietta St Lawrence, (5th Daughter of 3rd Earl of Howth)

c1. Sir Algernon Arthur St Lawrence Lee Guinness 1883–1954 (3rd Bart of Riverdene)

c2. Kenelm Lee Guinness, 1887–1937 (M.B.E., Won Tourist Trophy Isle of Man in 1913)

c3. Nigel Digby Lee Guinness, 1892–1970

Sir Edward Cecil Lee Guinness, 1847–1927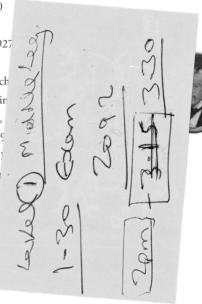
1919)

m. Adelaide M. Guinness, (daughter of Rich

Claude & Reginald who became involved in

c1. Sir Rupert Edward Cecil Lee Guinness,

c2. Hon. Arthur Ernest Guinness, 1876–19

c3. Hon. Walter Edward Guinness, 1880–1

in Cairo by the Zionist group Lehi, known

NEXT GENERATION

Sir Rupert Edward Cecil Lee Guinness,

m. Gwendolen Florence Mary Onslow, L

c1. Honor Dorothy Mary Guinness, 190

Frantisek Svejdar)

c2. Richard Guinness, 1906–1906

c3. Arthur Onslow Edward Guinness, 1912–1945, (Viscount Elveden, killed in action, m. Elizabeth Cecilia Hare)

c4. Patricia Florence Susan Guinness, 1918–2001 (m. Alan Lennox Boyd, 1904–1983)

c5. Lady Brigid Katherine Rachel Guinness, 1920–1995 (m. Frederick, Crown Prince of Prussia, 1911–1966; m2. Major Ness)

Arthur Ernest Guinness 1876–1949

m. Marie Clothilde Russell (1903)

c1. Aileen Sibell Mary Guinness, 1904–1999 (m1. Brinsley Sheridan Plunkett, m2. Valerian Stux Rylar)

c2. Maureen Constance Guinness, 1907–1998 (m1. Sir Sheridan Temple Blackwood Marquess of Dufferin & Ava; m2. Major Desmond Buchanan; m3. Judge John Cyril Maude

c3. Oonagh Guinness, 1910–1995 (m1. Philip Kindersley; m2. Dominick Browne, Baron Oranmore and Browne; m3. Miguel Ferrera)

Walter Edward Guinness 1880–1944 (1st Baron Moyne from 1932, MP for Bury St Edmunds, UK Minister for Agriculture, 1925–9)

m. Lady Evelyn Erskine, 1883–1939

c1. Bryan Walter Guinness, 1905–1992 (2nd Baron Moyne)

c2. Murtogh David Guinness, 1913–

c3. Grania Meve Rosaura Guinness, b1920– (m. Oswald Constantine John Phipps, 4th Marquess of Normanby)

NEXT GENERATION

Arthur Onslow Edward Guinness, 1912–1945 (Viscount Elveden, killed in action in Holland)

m. Elizabeth Cecilia Hare, b1914 (1936)

c1. Arthur Francis Benjamin Guinness, 1937–1992

c2. Lady Elizabeth Maria Guinness, b1937

c3. Hon. Henrietta Guinness, b1942

Bryan Walter Guinness, 1905–1992 (2nd Baron Moyne)

m. Diana Freeman-Mitford, 1910–2003 (1929)

c1. Jonathan Bryan Guinness (3rd Baron Moyne),

c2. Hon Desmond Walter Guinness, b1932

Arthur Francis Benjamin Guinness, 1937–1992 (3rd Earl of Iveagh, Member of Seanad Éireann)

m. Miranda Daphne Jane Smiley, b1940 (1963)

c1. Lady Louisa Jane Guinness, b1967

c2. Arthur Edward Rory Guinness, b1969 (4th Earl of Iveagh)

c3. Hon. Rory Michael Benjamin Guinness, b1974

Hon Desmond Walter Guinness, b1932 (of Leixlip Castle)

m. Marie Gabrielle Prinzessin von Urach, 1933–1989 (1954)

c1. Patrick Desmond Carl-Alexander Guinness, b1956

c2. Marina Guinness, b1957

Volume of Beer Produced at St James's Gate brewery from Lynch and Vaisey or Denisson

Data on volume of beer produced survives in brewing books and some figures are published in reports and the prospectus for the company flotation. Beer output figures are not as easily interpreted as might be expected. The gravity or strength of beer varied especially in the First World War period. Foreign Extra Stout was stronger than Extra Stout or porter. In more recent times figures are corrected for trade gravity as brewing is at high gravity for subsequent transport and liquor addition. There was also a measurement inconsistency in that at St James's Gate barrels were 32 imperial gallons until 1886 against the industry standard 36 gallons. Hogsheads were 52 gallon against industry standard of 54 gallon. Current measurement is in hectolitres and the conversion is 1.6 barrels to the hectolitre (100 litres). A standard barrel for excise duty was 36 gallons at a specific gravity of 1055.

Year	Barrels of Porter & Stout
1796	9,264 (Ale c700)
1799	11,487 (Ale 298)
1800	10,026
1815	66,672
1819	32,569
1820	27,374
1831	53,965
1836	74,010
1846	100,895
1865	331,176
1875	725,791
1885	1,357,000
1914	2,450,000
1918	920,000
1920	3,000,000
1930	2,199,000
1939	1,921,000
1945	1,930,000
1990	4.7 M Hl
2006	6.5 M Hl

Guinness barge on the Liffey.